THE
PROFIT
MACHINE

PUTTING THE FIVE PARTS OF PROFIT TO WORK

BY
LARRY EARNHART, Ph.D., M.B.A.

LARRY EARNHART

Published by:
Alchemy Business Consulting
Larry Earnhart
211 – 2623 Richmond Ave.
Victoria, BC V8R 4S8 Canada

While every attempt has been made to verify information provided in this book, neither the author nor the publisher assumes any responsibility for any errors, omissions or inaccuracies.

Any slights of people or organizations are unintentional. If advice concerning legal or related matters is needed, the services of a qualified professional should be sought. This book is not intended as a source of legal or accounting advice. You should be aware of any laws which govern business transactions or other business practices in your state or province.

The examples are not intended to represent or guarantee that everyone will achieve the same results. Each individual's success will be determined by his or her desire, dedication, effort, and motivation. There are no guarantees you will duplicate the results stated here, you recognize that any business endeavor has inherent risk for loss of capital.

Any reference to any persons or business, whether living or deceased, existing or defunct, is purely coincidental.

Earnhart, Larry, 1956-, author
The profit machine : putting the five parts of profit to work / by Larry Earnhart, Ph.D., M.B.A.

Includes bibliographical references.
Issued in print and electronic formats.
ISBN 978-0-9921095-2-3 (pbk.)
ISBN 978-0-9921095-3-0 (pdf)

1. Profit. I. Title.

HG4028.P7E27 2014
658.15'5
C2014-906696-1
C2014-906697-X

PRINTED IN THE UNITED STATES OF AMERICA

Table of Contents

Table of Figures

Acknowledgements

I would like to thank Leslie for being there for me and believing in me. She is my inspiration in everything I do.

Many thanks also to Ramona McKean and Dr. Alexandra Pett for their editing and proofreading expertise.

I also want to express my appreciation to Greg Thorne for his artwork and design on the cover.

Introduction

There is an innate human desire to be the master of your own destiny. When you start up your business you join the ranks of millions of other entrepreneurs who have taken that step by turning their ideas into action. Creating a new product or a new service and risking a steady job for the opportunity to be your own boss and strike out on your own is the backbone of the Free Enterprise system.

What distinguishes the successful entrepreneur from the failure? Many people think that luck is involved in success. It is true there is a role for serendipity in life but the reality is that opportunity knocks for those who are prepared to take advantage of it. As Oprah Winfrey once said, "Luck is preparation meeting opportunity."

In this book we will discuss a systematic way to make your business a successful business. But we are going to do this not by looking at your top-line revenue growth but at the real measure of success – profits. We are going to turn your business into a Profit Machine.

This book is not a one-concept book repeating the same idea over and over. This is an idea book. Use it to generate ideas that you can then use to take your business to the next level. The book is written for the entrepreneur who wants to learn more about business systems and how to make them work.

In MBA School they talk about BHAGs – Big Hairy Audacious Goals. But achieving those goals involves taking big leaps that can be incredibly risky. BHAGs are meant to be ground-breaking changes that can create whole new industries. The concepts I am talking about can be the source of your BHAGs.

I want you to think about this concept for your business. Break down the barriers you have created for yourself that prevent you from succeeding. Stop thinking about how your business will be 10% better next year and hopefully will finally turn a profit. Start thinking about taking your business to the next level. Start thinking of your business as a Profit Machine and then generate the processes that will get you to your goals and beyond.

Create a business that leverages your talent and ability not one where you are a one-person show doing everything yourself. Plan for success and soon opportunity will be breaking down your door, not just knocking at it.

Larry Earnhart
September 30, 2014

Chapter 1

Business & Profitability

Owning your own business may mean many things to you. You may have a product or service you really want to get to the marketplace. You may like that it provides you a job or that you can employ other people.

There are also social aspects to having a business, such as working with customers and working with employees. Perhaps the idea of social entrepreneurship, in which social problems are solved through business systems is appealing to you. Ultimately, being the boss gives you control over your own destiny.

Ultimately, owning a business is about making a profit. To some people the very idea of profit is a pejorative term. Some people feel that profit represents ruthless exploitation of the weak and powerless by Big Business.

Actually, if there are no profits there can be no business. Without profits there is no incentive to put in the hard work and time and trouble to start up and operate a business. Without profits there is not enough money coming in to compensate the investors and owners and to expand the business. Even a non-profit organization has to bring in enough cash to pay expenses.

To be an entrepreneur, first you need a business idea. Then you need to bring that idea into reality by starting your business. Then you need to nurture that business until it is self-sustaining. Finally, you need to make that business grow.

Some entrepreneurs spend months and even years with their idea, creating a business plan, nurturing it slowly. Others jump in there with no plan using the Ready, Fire, Aim approach. Either way can work as long as you just go ahead and begin.

At first you have big ideas for how your business will grow and prosper and envisioning yourself reaping the rewards of success. Then the hard work hits. Customers aren't lining up at the door and you need to go out prospecting for more but you are too busy with mundane tasks to do it. Your staff members are difficult to work with or quit unexpectedly. Clients don't pay on time. Vendors demand payment but fail to deliver on their promises.

Your nose becomes continually pressed to the grindstone and you are living day-to-day just hanging on, living out a never-changing existence where you are experiencing the same thing over and over and you are just barely hanging on.

Was this what you signed up for? Probably not. Your business may have stagnated at this point and you are stuck. You need to bring in a lot more customers so you can generate the money you need to just run the business not to mention putting your children through college, buying a new car or a new house, or having the retirement you long for.

How do you change things now? If you are stuck in a rut, how do you get unstuck? You need to analyze your business, figure out what is working and what is not.

To create change you need to create long-term goals that culminate in success. To accomplish this requires creation of a strategic plan setting goals for 1 year, 5 years and 10 years from now. What size business works for you? Do you want a $50,000 per year business? A $500,000 per year business or a $5,000,000 per year business or more?

The $5 Million Business

Suppose you have a small business you have been running out of your home earning about $50,000 a year in revenues. You started it up a couple of years ago hoping to turn it into a full-time operation so you could quit your job and become your own boss. You end up with $5,000 or maybe $10,000 in your pocket for the extra 10-20 hours per week you are putting into it on nights and weekends – which means you are earning $5 - $10 per hour, minimum wage at best.

Perhaps you have a larger business with $500,000 in sales, a storefront and an employee or two. You have moved out of your home, had success but are plateaued – you are taking $30,000 - $60,000 home but putting 60 hours a week into it, that still means you are earning $5 - $10 per hour, less than your staff makes for far more effort and dedication on your part.

You just KNOW you have a sure thing, the next Internet sensation. Your business just needs more customers, more exposure, and it will take off, right? There are many entrepreneurs who start out with rose-coloured glasses, thinking how their product just can't miss – all they have to do is get it out there and the customers will just run to their door with money in hand demanding to buy. Unfortunately, that's usually not how it works.

How do you generate enough income so you can grow and keep growing your business? If you are just barely hanging on or even if you are making a comfortable living how can you create enough earnings to expand and keep expanding?

Taking out loans or finding investors can be a solution. The negative aspect is that although you have more money for expansion, it comes at a price. The price is being beholden to someone; to having to pay her back (reducing your profitability in the meantime) and perhaps losing whatever collateral you put up if you fail.

Taking on a partner is another solution. Of course a partner will now have a say in running what is no longer just *your* business. If you give away too much, you may lose control over your business entirely.

By taking out a loan you owe someone else money (and interest). By accepting investment you give up ownership and control.

I'm not saying these are bad. On the contrary, taking on loans and investors at the right time can help a business take off. But the cost you pay may be more than you can afford right now and may compromise the payoff in the future.

You should maximize your business now. Squeeze everything you can out of it. Turn your business into a profit machine and when the time comes you will be expanding from a position of power. You will also be better able to dictate the terms of your loan or partnership rather than the other way around.

You should be frugal with your funds, your hard-earned revenues. Improve your profit margin by reducing your expenses. Improve your profit margin by improving your profit-creating activities. In this book we will explore how your profits break down into five components that you can manipulate to your advantage to turn your business into a Profit Machine.

When you start looking at your financial picture of your business you will find that profits are small numbers at the mercy of all the buying decisions you make each day. Every time you add staff, buy a chair, purchase a laptop or rent a storefront it comes out or your profits. Before you buy anything you must always ask yourself, "Can I support this expense with extra sales to cover the cost?"

Once you have your business on a sound financial footing, generating enough revenues to cover the cash flow and enough profits to allow for growth you can look towards growth.

Expansion is a critical time in a business. You need more help with sales or you don't have workers to keep up with manufacturing your product. You need office staff to handle bookkeeping. How much will it cost to expand? Every person you hire needs to be worth the cost to your business by generating larger profits.

Every level of growth requires more cash to run the business. Moving away from self-financing you now need to talk to investors about equity stakes in the business. You may go to the banks for a loan. Now you start to lose full control of your business as it starts to get too big for one person to manage.

The steps up to the $5 million business are higher. You need more people, you may need vehicles, warehouses, office space and manufacturing space. You will need to set up departments with mangers for each one.

Instead of a quick meeting to get everybody up to date you have planning meetings then your managers have their meetings. It can become too complex for one person to keep tabs on everything.

It is now the job of your senior managers to run the operation. Your job now becomes one of looking forward and creating the strategic plan instead of building what you have. This is a turning point for many entrepreneurs.

The changeover from day-to-day struggle and growth to planning and nurturing is the point where many entrepreneurs move on to the next idea. But first you have to get there with your Profit Machine.

Calculating Your Business Needs

Think about your business and personal goals. You will then estimate what it will take to generate the financial results you need to fulfill those goals.

List your personal life goals

_____

_____

_____

_____

_____

List your business goals

_____

_____

_____

_____

_____

How compatible are these goals with each other? What makes them workable or unworkable for you? How can you make your goals work together so you and your loved ones have the life you want to lead?

What size business are you looking for? Are you prepared for failure? What is your exit plan? Are you prepared for success? What happens if you reach your goals? What next?

How much money do you need per year to pay for your basic living needs?: $_____

This is the earnings you need from your business to allow you to quit your day job.

How much money do you want to earn for the lifestyle you dream of?: $_____

What percentage of Profit do you earn or do you think you will take out of your business as your earnings?: _____%

Divide the numbers above by that number to get the Revenues your business will need to earn for you to pay you what you need to earn = $50,000 / 10% Earnings = $500,000

Desired lifestyle earnings =
          $250,000 / 10% Earnings = $2.5 Million

These numbers represent the range of money that your busines will have to earn in sales revenues for you to generate enough money for you to live on.

Does your business make this kind of earnings? If not how will you get there? Are you being realistic about your profit margin?

Figure 1. Calculate Your Business Needs

Your Legacy

When it is time to close down your business what will you walk away from? If it fails you will have to liquidate assets and pay off loans as best you can, perhaps declare bankruptcy. What if you are successful? Will you have created enough value that your business can be sold for a profit or handed down to your children as a way to generate retirement income?

The profitability of your business defines the value. In accounting terms it is what is called "Retained Earnings" on the corporate balance sheet. If you try to sell the business the value that you can put it on the market for it depends on the amount of profits you have earned over its lifetime.

This flies in the face of the reasonable desire to reduce taxes. Who wants to pay more money to the government? Many business owners will try to claim whatever they can possibly justify as a business expense to reduce taxable profits. So they buy toys such as luxury or sporty vehicles or golf club memberships or put family vacation travel down as business expenses. As long as they don't get audited by the IRS or Revenue Canada they feel that is OK.

Realize that if you join this club you may actually be cheating yourself in the long run. If you intend to sell your business someday it is the lifetime accumulation of profit that determines the selling price along with the desirability of the product and the current and potential customer base. Talk to your accountant before you buy that BMW as a "business expense."

Chapter 2

Profits vs. Revenues

Whenever we talk about the size of a company we usually talk about it in terms of its revenues. How much money did it bring in from sales? We need to realize that revenues and profits are distinctly different. Why don't we talk about profits instead? Perhaps because revenues are simpler to deal with. Sales are pretty obvious and don't fluctuate as much over time as profits do.

The amount of profits your business earns depends upon many factors. In a large corporation there may have been a big layoff resulting in early retirement payouts (a "special charge" against earnings).

There may have been a one-time sale of assets that bump up the profits exceptionally high. But concentrating solely on revenues leads to the quarterly-based decision-making that the large corporations use to shore up their stock prices. A case in point:

> I was always amazed at the large Fortune 500 Company I once worked for that insisted that we meet monthly sales revenue targets no matter what so that the stock analysts would be satisfied and the stock price was boosted.

> What actually happened was that the salespeople for our division would have "fire sales" to pressure our customers to buy more product than we were able to produce since we were at full production capacity.

The customers couldn't use the product right away since they already had their raw materials hoppers filled up. They would just take it at a later date resulting in reduced future sales and reduced profits for my company. In other words our annual profits actually decreased in order to prop up short-term corporate revenues.

Nobody seemed to see the fallacy here – short-term revenue gains vs. long-term profitability.

Since this approach satisfied the investment analysts the CEO was praised for his ability to deliver results even if they were the wrong results for the long run.

As small business owners we sell our products or services, take the revenues generated and put the money into our checking accounts. We then pay our bills from those checking accounts and hope there is enough money left over to pay ourselves a salary.

If we do pay ourselves then we may just end up loaning it right back to the business later when things slow down again and we can't pay our bills. Or we may "plow the money back into the business" instead of paying ourselves. This is a warning to ourselves that the business is not self-sustaining unless it is indeed expanding and needs capital for growth.

I would like you to turn the viewpoint of financial operations around and instead of letting Revenues drive the business – make Profit be the driver instead.

How much money do you need to earn to make your business viable for your needs? If you have quit your day job and are doing this full-time how much income are you replacing with your business? How long can you go before the bank forecloses on your home? Or if you are doing this on the side how much money makes it worth all the aggravation and the time you are missing out with family?

When starting up our businesses we are told that we have to "pay our dues" and forgo any profits until we "make it." And until we start generating enough sales to start covering our expenses that is true. Except that we should be looking at profitability from the start.

How do you do that? By structuring your operation so that you put profit ahead of revenues. Any buying decision should be based on the return on the investment made. Realize that any expenditure you make will reduce the amount of money going into your pocket unless you earn more revenues to cover it.

If you don't have more money coming in than going out when will that change? You have a breakeven point where your revenues equal your fixed costs for raw materials and manufacturing labor plus your overhead costs (you and your office and staff). For every widget you sell beyond that point you earn a profit.

Instead of trying to sell more and more products to generate more and more revenues first determine how much you need to sell to make what you want in profits. Once you have a profit goal you can figure out what sales you need to generate it. Let your profits drive your revenues not your revenues drive your profits.

Introducing Handyman Joe

Meet Handyman Joe, a small business owner like yourself. He will provide a real-life based demonstration of how turn a business into a Profit Machine.

The financial results used are simplified versions of actual results. This means that results won't be as tidy and neat as if they had just been made up for the book but should be more realistic when comparing them to your own situation. The Appendix has a fuller outline of Joe's business and the financial numbers behind it.

Handyman Joe bought an existing handyman franchise business that had been making small but reasonable profits in his hometown area .Although Joe was a home handyman and had misgivings that he was not a professional craftsman the franchisors had assured him otherwise.

They told him that it was not important that he have experience actually doing craftsman-level work. They claimed that in their experience craftsmen actually did not do well as franchisees but managers and entrepreneurs did because of their experience managing people and running operations.

Joe had been working for others his entire life and having been a mid-level manager at his old firm before he was laid off felt ready to strike out on his own. He was excited at the prospect.

He bought the business from two brothers. One brother had become quite ill and they were no longer able to manage their business so it seemed to be a reasonable reason to sell. They had purchased the business from the original franchisees five years earlier and all the financial records were available for review.

Joe felt that he had a strong basis to purchase the business. After showing him the financial numbers his accountant concurred. Joe went ahead and bought the business.

What is Profit?

Many of us small business owners look at the monthly balance in our company checkbook as the indicator of how well or how poorly our business is doing. If we have more at the end of the month than at the start, we have earned a profit and if we have less, we have a loss. The problem is that while this approach may work for the solopreneur or a very small operation it breaks down when you get to a certain size.

*Profits Are What Are Left Over After All the
Expenses Have Been Paid*

Your profits can become an elusive figure once your business has equipment and cars, loans, accounts payable and accounts receivable. You have to start to think ahead and consider what upcoming expenses you have rather than when your customers will actually pay you. Otherwise you can easily end up out of money and having to close the doors. No matter what, you should be very aware of your revenues and expenses and be in control of them at all times.

Where Do Profits Come From?

First let's start with Revenues. Of course you know what Revenues are – they are all the money you bring into your business from selling your product or service to your customers. It is the money you earn by fulfilling your customers' needs.

I look at this as filling your company cookie jar. The cookies represent the money you've earned from selling your products.

That is only part of the picture though. In order to run a business you have to pay for the business to run. You may rent a space, lease or purchase a vehicle, buy a telephone system, a computer, some office furniture, perhaps hire an employee or two. If you make a product rather than provide a service you have to pay for the raw materials and for the cost of putting it together. There is also insurance expense. If, after all that, you have profit left over, you of course have to pay taxes on it.

Revenues

These are all expenses and you can think of these as cookies being taken back out of your cookie jar. If you have too many expenses you

Figure 2. Revenues are the Cookies in Your Cookie Jar

may have no cookies left or you may even owe cookies for expenses you can't pay now.

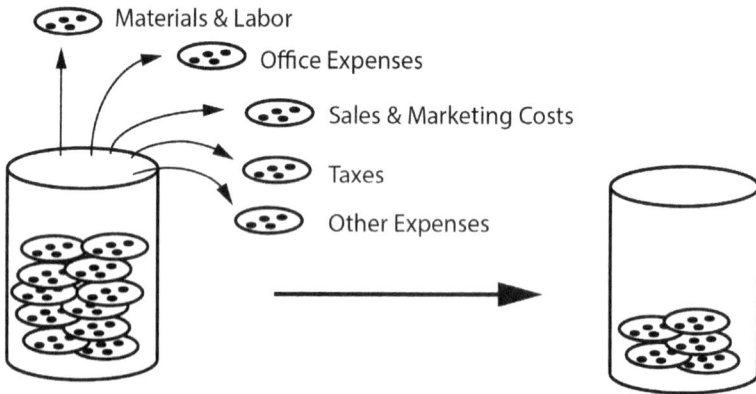

Materials & Labor
Office Expenses
Sales & Marketing Costs
Taxes
Other Expenses

Revenues - Expenses

Profits

Figure 3. Profits Are What's Left After Expenses Are Paid

Many small business owners start out financing their businesses by maxing out their credit cards, cashing in retirement accounts, remortgaging their houses or borrowing from family and friends.

Loans provide necessary the liquid capital (read: cash) to keep your business afloat until you have made enough sales to cover your expenses and to pay you a salary. If not, you won't be able to pay your bills and you will have to cease operations.

If you run out of money you may end up with a ruined credit rating, ruined family relationships, no retirement funds and a house foreclosed upon. A good, sound business plan and a good, solid product or service and proper planning and analysis help to create a solid, growing business.

There are a number of tools you can use to help analyze your business. These tools are used to compare the financial results of one month to the next and to compare your business with another one in the same industry. One of these is Profit Margin.

Profit Margin one of the most useful business ratios. You can calculate Profit Margin from your monthly or yearly accounting

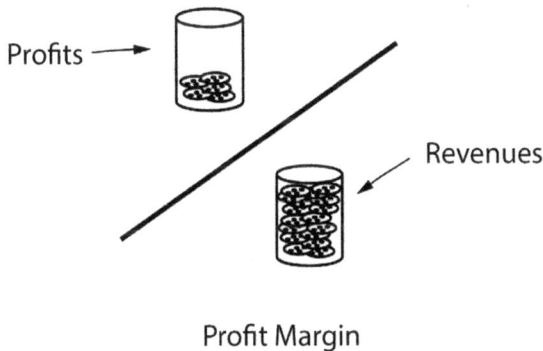

Profit Margin

Figure 4. Profit Margin Defined

statements. If you use computer software to handle your books you can call up a report and automatically generate the number for any time period you want. You can use Profit Margin to determine how efficient your business is in creating profits. Ratios like this tend to remain fairly stable over time as long as the business is operating under fairly stable conditions.

If the Profit Margin changes it can give you a head's-up to

A. How much are your Revenues?

- What is your product and how much does it sell for?

- How many do you sell per month?

B. What are your expenses?

- Manufacturing costs of materials and labor?

- Overhead costs of rent, utilities, insurance, marketing, administrative salaries, interest on loans, etc.?

Subtract B. from A   A – B = C   = Your Profits

Divide C by A   C / A   = Your Profit Margin

Figure 5. Calculate Your Profit Margin

investigate what is different from before. The Profit Margin can also be used to project how much profit you could earn given different amounts of revenue for planning purposes.

Using our cookies and cookie jar example, you can see Profit Margin represented below.

The profit margin is a measure of the efficiency of your business. You can calculate this number from the monthly or annual totals of sales and net profit. This ratio can be used in turn to calculate expected sales revenues in the future.

In the next five chapters we will break Profit down into the five component Parts of Profit and look at each one individually. We will look at what you can do to create a high performance operation that can generate all the money you need to meet your business and personal goals.

Each one of the Parts of Profit touch on a major aspect of running a business. In fact the entire scope of Business operations falls within them.

Chapter 3

The Five Parts of Profit

I'm going to take you on a journey. On this journey we will reverse-engineer Profits breaking it down into its five component parts. These five parts represent the individual pieces you can manipulate separately and synergistically to turn your business into a Profit Machine.

First of all, look at our cookie jar drawings below:

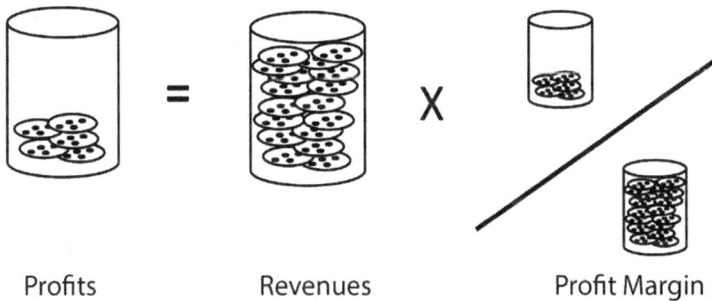

Figure 6. Profits Are Revenues Times Profit Margin

We learned in the previous chapter that Profit Margin comes from dividing the amount of your profits by the amount of your revenues. Now we will turn the equation around and take out Profit Margin. I know it sounds like a circular argument, like defining a word in the dictionary by the word itself but just bear with me. `Profit Margin is one of the Five Parts of profit that we will learn to manipulate in our Profit Machine.

That leaves Revenues as the other part of this equation. What are the Revenues of your business? As we discussed before in this book, they are the result of your customers spending their hard-earned money for your product or service (I'm just going to say "product" from now on instead of the unwieldy term, "product or service").

Ultimately, what we want to do as businesspersons is to influence people so they will want to purchase our products. We want people to understand how our products will benefit them. We want people to buy and keep on buying those products. By giving us their business we will earn the money in profits to expand our businesses, pay our bills, put our kids through college, enjoy our retirement and whatever else we desire as the return on our investment.

Revenues breaks down into two parts and each part further breaks down into two more. When we are done we will have four components from Revenues and one from Profit Margin adding up to the Five Parts of Profit.

There are two ways to calculate Revenues. The first is to simply add up all the dollars you've earned in sales for the month. The way we will use in this book is to multiply the Number of Customers you have by the average amount of money they spend – what is called Customer Value.

You may have heard of the term, "Lifetime Customer Value." This is the amount of money a customer will spend over the lifetime of the business. Here we will talk about revenues in monthly or yearly terms.

Think of going to the grocery store. You go there a certain number of times a year – perhaps averaging once per week. You spend roughly the same amount of money each week. The grocery store knows on average how many times per month or per year customers visit the store and on average how much they spend.

This information gives the grocery store powerful information about its customers' buying habits. Store management uses this information to forecast how much inventory to keep for stocking shelves and to know how to prepare for seasonal purchases.

The total amount of money you and the other customers spend

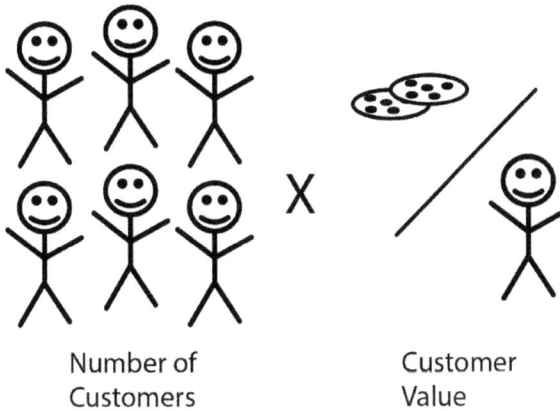

Number of Customers   Customer Value

Figure 7. Revenues are the Number of Customers
Times the Amount They Spend

at the grocery store over the course of a month is the monthly revenue for the store – the cookies going into their cookie jar. Now grocery stores have very slim profit margins – less than 1-2% of their revenues actually ends up as profit. They keep very close track of that number among others and are very quick to respond if it changes in any way up or down.

New expenditures come out of profits unless you generate more sales to pay for them. Divide proposed expenditures by the profit margin and you will learn how much it costs in terms of additional sales to pay for them. This shows you how Profit Margin and Revenues are related. It also gives you an understanding of how some businesses get in trouble thinking that an extra expenditure is not that big a deal when in fact it is.

For example, a large supermarket may take in $25 million in revenues per year which calculates out to $68,000 per day from about 2,000 customers.

A 2% profit margin means $500,000 in profits per year. ($25,000,000 times 2%) equalling $1,360 per day.

In order to pay for a new deli case costing $10,000 the store needs to get its customers to buy an additional $500,000 in products over the lifetime of that deli case. (Calculated by dividing $10,000 by 2%). Otherwise profits decline by $10,000.

If the store were to hire an additional employee earning $25,000 in wages and benefits per year it would require earning $1,500,000 or more in additional annual revenue. (Calculated by dividing $25,000 by 2%) to keep the same profit margin. If no additional revenues are generated to compensate for the expense, the store's profits drop by $25,000 per year.

Activities vs. Results

When you think about your customers and the amount of money they have spent for your products you are looking backwards in time. These are events that have already happened. When you tally up your monthly revenues you find you have had a certain number of customers who have spent a certain amount of money with you.

You cannot influence these numbers at this point because you are looking at events in the past. So, how do you change these numbers in the future? How do you get more customers to spend more money on your products next month and the month after that?

> In my time as a financial advisor I was held accountable on a day-to-day basis for my results in building my business. It wasn't based on the number of clients I served or the amount of money I brought in (OK, I was accountable for those too, but in a secondary way). I was taught to measure my activities not my results. My activities were counted as how many times I made a "Good Contact" with a prospective customer.

> A Good Contact was made when I talked to a customer over the phone or face-to-face, brought a financial product to her attention and asked for an order. If I made 25 Good Contacts per day and did that consistently day after day I knew that I would be successful in the industry because a certain measurable percentage of those contacts would eventually turn into sales.

Think about this. This is a very powerful idea:

You Only Have Control Over Your Activities
Not Over Your Results

This relatively simple concept was an epiphany for me and allowed me to understand my role as a salesperson. As we go through this book concentrate on what you can actually control. Don't focus on the RESULTS of your activities as they are beyond your control. Instead, keep performing the activities that will lead to success.

Just like the number of customers or the amount of sales you've generated you can't control your customers' buying decisions. What you can control is what you say and do in your contacts with prospective customers through the sales and marketing actions you undertake. You also control how you deal with your customers through your customer service levels

Number of Customers

Generating customers is a process. The number of customers you have is the result of your Marketing and Sales efforts.

Of the 7 billion people on this planet relatively few need, want or even have the money to buy your product. Even corporate giants like Microsoft, Apple and Facebook cannot lay claim to that many prospective customers no matter how popular their products are.

Figure 8. Number of Customers

Those people who have some likelihood of making a purchase of your product at some point or another are called your demographic. You want your demographic to learn about your product and your business. This is called Marketing and you need to spend your time and money working within your demographic group.

Your Target Market is the specific niche group or groups within your demographic that you narrow down your focus to reach. In fact, finding an unserved niche within your demographic is the way many small business owners have found to grow and prosper.

For example, if you are a yoga studio owner in Victoria, BC your demographic may be 25% men and 75% women age 20 – 65 (Natural Marketing Institute (NMI), 2008). One of the latest trends in yoga is the Hot Yoga studio, a takeoff of Bikram Yoga where the studio is kept quite warm and humid. Because of these conditions your target market niche may be older men who want to loosen up muscles tightened up golfing or playing seniors' hockey (Ottawa Insight, 2014). This is a niche market that may not even know needs your services until these men hear how well your product works for them.

If you sell cosmetics then you're likely talking about females older than 10-12 years tapering off at perhaps 70-80 years. Your market niche could then be teen-age girls you are producing a line of lipsticks in bright colors in special shades and textures.

When looking at the target market for marketing Nerf guns the users are boys 8 – 18. You are not selling directly to those boys though are you? Who buys the guns? Is it the user? It is the parents and grandparents your marketing needs to appeal to in addition to the users who will ask them to buy the products.

For the small entrepreneur this is where the ability to be nimble and to be small enough to take advantage of a niche comes into play. The larger a corporation becomes the less able it is to serve small niche markets. A niche product can often be sold for a higher price because of heightened demand from a smaller number of people than the large companies can afford to market to. The opportunity is for the small business to be able to take advantage of the ability to make a profit with a much smaller number of customers.

This is the area where the entrepreneur creates change, upsets markets and creates entire new product categories. The concepts of Facebook and Twitter were not even thought of by the big media companies yet they have now almost completely overtaken the telecoms. These were started by small entrepreneurs and grew and grew.

Prospects and Customers

Your Customers all started out as Prospective Customers at one point. A Prospect is someone who has heard about your company or your product but for various reasons has not bought anything from you yet. Prospecting is another term for Marketing.

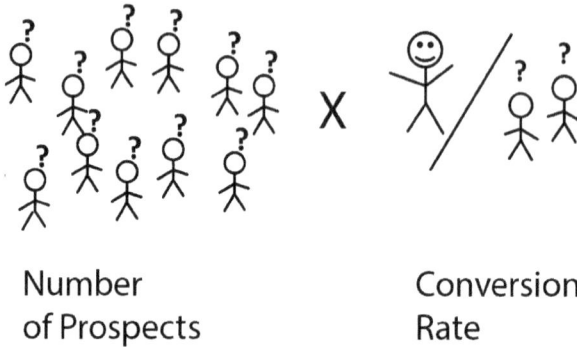

| Number of Prospects | Conversion Rate |

Figure 9. Converting Your Prospects into Customers

The rate that Prospective Customers (Prospects) are converted into Customers is called the Conversion Rate. The process of converting Prospects into Customers is called Sales. The Number of Customers you have is the number of Prospects times the Conversion Rate they are turned into Customers.

Your Prospects may be in different stages of buying readiness:

- Heard of you but uninterested in buying
- Heard of you but interested in a competitor's product
- Shopping around but wanting to buy either your or a competitors' product
- Wants to buy your product but not ready to buy now
- Money in hand ready to buy right now

However, until they actually purchase your product they are still Prospects.

The Sales Funnel

One way to understand the sales process is to use the Sales Funnel concept. A sales funnel is a tool to keep track of people scattered along the sales process. It is called a funnel because at each stage the number gets smaller and smaller. Eventually, you get to the number of people who pass through the bottom and end up as customers.

At the top of your sales funnel is the pool of potential customers. Those who might find your product useful or worthy of purchase can be termed "Suspects." This group are those people who don't know about your product yet but are within your product's demographic group.

Your marketing efforts are designed to reach these Suspects to get them to move further into your funnel and become Prospects. You can then use your sales process to convert Prospects into Customers.

Filling the sales funnel is a constant process. As you convert Prospects into Customers you need to keep refilling your funnel with new Prospects otherwise you will quickly run out of people to convert. To get the word out to your target market, you may rely on traditional marketing such as newspaper, TV, Radio, etc.

You may rely on networking, word of mouth or social media. As more people get to know you and learn about your great product and fantastic service your marketing may turn into a word of mouth campaign generating endless referrals from your happy customers.

Generating Prospects and turning them into Customers depends first on people hearing about you, your company and your product through your Marketing efforts. When a prospect trusts you enough to feel that your product will do what he wants it to do at a price he thinks is worth the value he perceives the product will give him he will buy it.

Marketing & Sales are About Earning
the Customer's Trust

Without some level of trust why would anybody want to part with her money on the chance that your product might work as you

The Sales Funnel

Figure 10. The Sales Funnel

say it will? Would you trust someone who just walked up and asked you to buy his car? Or to marry her? Of course not. You must trust him or her first. And learning to trust starts out with familiarity.

When you hear about something often enough, from friends and family and from other sources you start to feel that you can trust this vendor and her product. Familiarity, in the form of Social Proof breaks down the barriers to trust.

This familiarity concept carries over into famous personalities which is why you see sports and entertainment figures paid large sums of money to hawk products – they have high credibility even though we don't know them personally.

Customer Value

What is a customer worth to your business? How much your customers are spending on your products? Customer Value is the Price that people pay times the Number of times they return to buy from you again.

There are two components to Customer Value: Price and Number of Repeat Sales. Price means not just the price of a particular product but the total amount of money that is paid for an entire sale.

Price could include upsold items like you see at a fast-food restaurant when you are asked if you want fries or a larger drink with your order. It could include bundling together a package of items in a set or it could lead to repeat sales with sequels to a book or updated products. It could just be the basket of goods you buy at the grocery store.

Each visit she might have a quite varied list of items in her basket but over time that basket will average out to a certain amount of money. Perhaps a particular customer averages spending $100 once per week at the store. That means that over 52 weeks the annualized customer value is $5,200. The lifetime customer value calculated over 20 years is over $100,000.

The price you set for your product gives customers an idea of the value you set for your product. A high price relative to your competitors tells prospective customers that you consider your product to be higher quality than the average. However, a lower price could mean that your product is cheap or inferior or that you are willing to bargain.

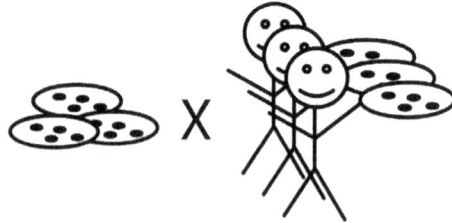

Price   Number of Repeat Sales

Figure 11. Customer Value

A business might have a product that is a one-time purchase item, for example, a book. You buy it, you read it and there is no reason to purchase another copy of the same book from the author, unless you buy another one for a friend as a gift. This means the lifetime customer value for a $15 book is $15. If the author writes a sequel that the customer buys because they like the first one the lifetime customer value is $30.

If the author is Stephen King you might like his writing so much you buy all 54 of his books (as of this writing) and your lifetime customer value could be $250 - $1,000 depending on whether you buy paperback or hardcover editions, plus some books that have more than one version. You might hate his writing and buy one book and never finish it and your lifetime customer value would be $5.

The items you can manipulate or influence are the prices you charge for your products and the desire of the customer to come back and buy again.

The value you give to your customers in the performance of your product and the experience the customers have dealing with you determines whether they come back to buy from you again. Repeat business is a function of customer service.

Repeat sales occur when the customer decides to return to your business to buy again. A dissatisfied customer won't return and in fact will tell others what a bad place it is to their friends and family. This negative passion drives a strong desire to let others know and is can be far greater than the positive glow from a happy customer telling their friends how great you are.

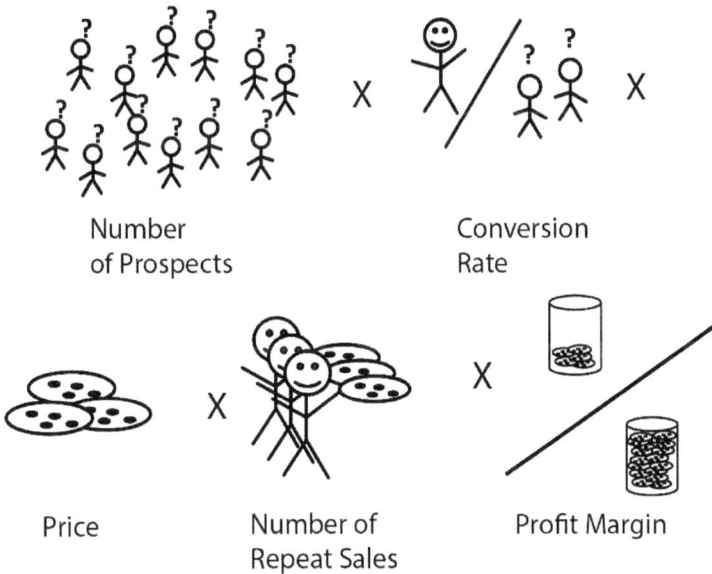

Figure 12. The Five Parts of Profit

As we will see, many businesses say they offer exemplary customer service but few actually provide it. You may be assuming that you are an expert at generating goodwill with your customers without knowing that the opposite is true.

Now we have the Five Part of Profit. In the next 5 chapters we will go over each Part in detail showing you how to create your own Profit Machine.

Chapter 4

Number of Prospects – Marketing

How do people learn about your products? Prospecting is the process of making people aware of and interested in your product. It is a Marketing process where you are telling people, "I am here, I am here, I am here" trying to get their attention amidst a sea of other marketers doing the same thing for all the other products out there as well. It starts the process of trust building that you need to be able to get people to spend their hard-earned money on your product.

Marketing is also designed to get people to see the uniqueness of your business and the niche your products fit into. This is called branding. By emphasizing this uniqueness in a way that your demographic will remember you and your products you create "Top Of Mind Awareness" or TOMA.

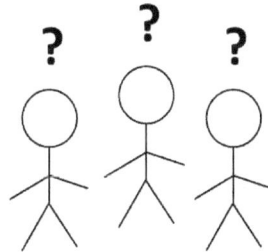

Figure 13. Prospects

TOMA means that when the customer determines he or she is ready to buy your product it is YOUR product that she is most likely to buy. It means that you and your product are the first thing the customer thinks of when the time comes to buy. This is the reason why traditional marketing relies so much on interruption and repetition to get the point across. It creates a memory pattern inside your mind that is triggered by a stimulus: a need, an emotion, a sight, sound or smell – generating TOMA in response.

Marketing may take many forms. There is traditional marketing: Newspaper, Radio, TV, Flyers. Mass media, mass marketing that is by its nature unable to specifically target individuals but may be able to reach general groups that approximate your target demographic.

There are billboards, team sponsorships from Little League to professional, bus bench ads, bus ads, ads on shopping carts and cars door hangers and lawn signs. Even tattoos. Pretty much anyplace a logo can be stuck on there will be ad copy not far behind.

There is the phenomenon of social media. This can be considered a form of mass media that bypasses traditional marketing methods using word of mouth to generate interest. Using Facebook Twitter, Pinterest, LinkedIn and the many other social media brands requires an investment of time more than money.

Many commercials on TV and in the mass media appear pretty pointless and may not even seem to have anything to do with the product they are selling. The key is in linking their product with a feeling that creates a trigger in the customer's mind associating it with something good – for an automobile it could be family safety or enjoying the sporty ride; in a truck, toughness; for beer, pretty girls and the illusion that the two are somehow interrelated. The association may not even be a positive one – it is just the repetition that is important and the association is made to a jarring situation or image or sound.

By creating this memory track in your mind you can't help but be triggered by it when you hear a familiar sound such as the five-note McDonald's jingle (did you hear it play in your mind just now?). We also see so many ads so many times every day that we are used to filtering them out and to get your attention they need to grab you – interrupt what your are doing so you pay attention enough for it to filter through into your consciousness.

This traditional branding process is expensive and only the larger businesses can afford to use it at the level required to truly, indelibly etch their names upon your brain. On a smaller scale you want to find a way to get your name out in front of your demographic audience within your target market zone – perhaps in your city or within a certain section of the internet. This can be done through radio, local TV or flyer drops, which, while costly can be effective in a local market.

Using the Internet can be tricky, especially in light of recent anti-spam laws, very good quality spam filters and general antipathy by the public towards unsolicited marketing messages. A relatively recent development is called Content Marketing – giving away valuable information through Blogs, downloads, webinars, etc. that drive the potential customer to want more from you and to want to pay for extra valuable information.

On the small scale, social contact through networking groups, BNI (Business Networking International) groups, friends and family to get the word out are where many people start. Social media can be used as well but the interaction is less personal. Although it can reach a much larger audience than traditional networking the quality of the interactions is not as strong. It is necessary to use a higher frequency and amount of time to connect with potential customers.

Social networking is a loose kind of networking where you reach people through a relay of contacts. The idea is that your message is appealing to people who see it and they pass it on to their friends who pass it on to their friends and on and on until it goes, "viral."

If your post or message goes viral it can potentially reach millions of people virtually overnight. However, it takes time and effort to be posting relevant commentary that is noticeable enough to catch popular attention.

Popular attention does not, however, ensure increased sales. As many businesses with popular TV commercials have found, just because many people find the advertisement interesting it does not necessarily translate into more sales. The largest corporations reach hundreds of millions of people with their marketing. That marketing may cost hundreds of millions of dollars annually just to gain a fraction of a percentage point of market share from their competitors. You, as a small business owner might reach a small neighborhood of a few dozen people by networking or a few hundred neighbors with a weekly newspaper ad.

Look at the demographic group that is likely to buy your product and determine how many sales you are likely to make and what it would take to get to the widest audience you could get. The more specifically you can target your audience the less money you will spend on deaf ears.

> Earlier we talked about Handyman Joe's handyman business. His marketing activities target an area with 350,000 residents – around 60,000 single-family homes. His target market is people who are 35-55 years old, own their own homes and have over $50,000 in family income. Certainly, non-homeowners and people older and younger than that can use his services and do call up for appointments but the main group of people who he makes the greatest profit from are from that target group.

> By studying the statistics of who his best customers are to find out who uses his services Joe determined the best use of his marketing funds is to target that group of homeowners. By concentrating on this target group he

has a much better chance of success and his marketing dollars are spent more effectively, lowering the cost of customer acquisition.

One thing Joe realized is that in his Sales presentations he most often talks to the wife and she is often the decision-maker on accepting contracts with his business.

Benefits vs. Features

Entrepreneurs often get caught up in telling potential customers all about the features of their product. An example of this is in the software industry where feature after feature is added to entice customers with grand products that will do everything except slice bread. These features are often never used because they are too complicated to use no matter how good they sound.

Features are not the reason people will buy a product, however. They buy something to fulfill a need and to make them feel better. Think about going to buy a car. Why do you think the automobile makers spend so much time and energy on styling and comfort?

Sure they put in lots of features and they market them too but when most of us go car-shopping we may spend a lot or a little time looking at different models and prices and gas mileages but what happens when it is time to buy?

We sit in it. We take it for a drive – maybe even literally kick the tires. We listen to the sound of the engine. We feel the comfort level of the ride and the noise level of the cabin. Maybe we don't like how the turn signals work or the way the seatback sits. We may be concerned we cannot find the color or body style we want.

The ultimate decision is not based on the features, it is based on the base appeal to our egos. If we are a 50-something guy maybe it is the feel of a red Porsche appeals to our 2nd childhood. Or knowing that the boxy van will keep our kids safe and get them to the game on time.

Notice that many commercials for small cars are trying to appear "hip" and "edgy" with shots of young kids partying and playing "hip" and "edgy" music and lots of odd cutaway shots. They are trying to sell these young drivers the first cars they will own. By being the first car maker these younger adults buy from they hope to create an ongoing relationship and continued brand loyalty when they buy cars in the future.

Think about, "What emotion does my product appeal to?" Not, "What kinds of stuff does it have attached?"

Referral Marketing

Have you ever bought a product you liked so well that you just had to tell your friends about it? Did they then go out and buy that product as well? Do people talk about your product that way to their friends and family?

Taking buying advice from friends and family is called Social Proof and tapping into this free marketing process is key to improving your profits.

What would happen to your profits if you had a veritable army of loyal customers beating the bushes to tell others about your product? What would happen to your marketing and advertising costs? The first goes up while the second goes down. Having a referral-based business is the Holy Grail for the small business owner. A referral is up to 15 times more likely to do business with you than a cold prospect. (Securities Industry Association)

In Chapter 7 we will talk about Customer Rewards Programs as a way to get customers to come back again and again. In the same fashion a referral program can get customers to gladly hand over into your care their most trusted friends and family members as referrals. If each of your customers sent you two referrals and if only one of them bought your product but referred two more people your business would take off.

The prospects who you meet this way have heard good things about you and they have are ready to hear more by the time they meet you. As we will learn in the next chapter, trust is the key to making a sale and Social Proof provided by a referral from a satisfied customer makes a trusting relationship that much easier to attain.

To create a referral-based business requires a good, solid product and exceptional service. There is another piece to it though. You have to establish a trusting relationship with your customers. They must feel that you have their best interests at heart. This is done by treating them right – a high quality product that does what you say it does, one that is fully guaranteed and provides them with an experience that they would like their friends to experience as well.

Certainly some people will find your product and service so overwhelmingly wonderful that they will spontaneously spread the word to others on your behalf. To make your business based on referrals you cannot rely on that. You need to ask people to make those referrals to you.

The way to generate referrals is to ask your customers,

> *"Who else do you know who would like to receive the same kind of service I provide for you?"*

Many salespeople are reluctant to ask because they feel they are intruding or being "pushy." You are indeed being pushy if you are asking someone you don't have trust with or someone who doesn't feel that they have received an appropriate level of customer service. You are not being pushy to ask someone you have a good relationship with.

Although you, like many others, might find it difficult you have to <u>ask</u> if you are going to <u>receive</u>. Even if you have a business where relatively close relationships may form with clients such as being a financial advisor or a lawyer you still have to ask. In the financial services industry 86% of surveyed customers would refer their broker to their friends, yet only 12% had ever been ASKED. (Securities Industry Association)

By telling them you are going to ask for referrals up front you are setting expectations. When the relationship has deepened your customers will not be surprised when you ask for referrals. They will already be thinking about who would be worthy of being referred to you.

One of the best ways to start off a business relationship with a new client is to tell her,

> *"I get paid in two ways. One is by your payment for my service (or product). The other is that assuming you are satisfied with my service you will recommend me to other people you know."*

When do you actually ask for a referral? Usually it is best after you have achieved something positive in the eyes of your customer. After the sale or the service has been completed, after you have done a favor for him, after you have resolved a customer complaint for her. At this point your customer is in a positive frame of mind towards you. Why would they not want to help you out in return?

I know of some professionals who badger their clients, handing them a piece of paper and practically demanding they write down the names of their friends and family. This is a heavy-handed tactic that may backfire generating ill-will rather than good. There are better ways to accomplish the goal. The problem is that even under the best of intentions people will forget.

Another approach is to prepare a letter or even a business card that the customer will sign <u>her own</u> name to telling her friends how much the she enjoyed your product and would appreciate that they give their business to you in turn. This is a very powerful form of social proof. Your evangelists especially will be happy to do this.

Referral Rewards Programs

In the Referral Rewards Program you give a reward or a perk in return for the referral names. For five names a customer will receive a discount on their next purchase or even cash back. In the 2-sided reward the referred person also receives a perk for buying the product.

In order to prevent people from giving you names of unlikely prospects you want to set up your program so that the perks for the customer and the referred friend are not doled out unless the friend purchases your product.

What might appeal to your customers as a perk? Would they find motivation in some cash rebates? How about free product or discounts? Maybe a free movie or car wash, a TV or iPod or even a car detailing.

I know a realtor who will give a $1,000 gift for any referral that leads to a sale of a property. I know a contractor who gives 10% of the price of the job to the referrer. How about a gift to a charity you both support?

The reward should be something that is motivating to the recipient to want to get it but not so it bankrupts you or reduces your profits instead of generating more. Your ROI should be greater than your standard marketing ROI. In fact the rewards you give could simply be recognition and a thank you.

In any event once a referral funnel starts up and as long as you feed it with your excellent product and fantastic customer service it will continue and allow you to grow without spending huge amounts of your revenues (thereby increasing your profits) on sales and marketing.

> *When You Receive a Referral it is in Your Best Interest to Act on it Immediately.*

You may have to wait until the client talks to the person she is referring but do not let it sit on your desk until you get around to it. That is a sure way to turn lemonade into lemons.

This is a favored client who likes you well enough to give you access to the most important people in his life. How would you feel if the tables were turned? You give a businessperson a list of friends, you tell them that this great entrepreneur will call them and make their lives better and then what?

Nothing. No call, no contact. Maybe after a couple of weeks a call or an email comes in. How do you feel now? Do you even want to do business with that guy anymore yourself?

Instead, when you get a referral you call them up immediately, and use the person's name who referred her to you.

> *"Hi Mr. Jones, I'm Joe Smith of Joe's Handyman Services. Jane Doe told me that you might have an interest in my services and suggested I call you. I'd like to set up a time to meet for a quick coffee so I can tell you about my business and learn about how I can be of value to you."*

Notice that Joe has told Mr. Jones about his source. This is a key to establishing credibility and starting the process of trust-building with your potential client. Since Mr. Jones knows and trusts Jane Doe he is willing to transfer some of that trust to you. You want to set up an appointment so you add,

> *"I have some time available at 10:00 Monday morning or 1:00 Tuesday afternoon, which works better for you?"*

When setting appointments give a choice of two suggested times. If they can't make it either time offer another or ask when they would be available.

It is better not to ask yes or no questions such as, "

> *How would you like to meet sometime?"*

Asking for specific times for a meeting makes it an either-or choice. It is easier to say no to a yes or no question. If you give specific times it shows the customer that you are busy and a busy person is a successful person.

No matter what happens, it is imperative that you

send a thank-you note back to the referral source as soon as you can. You do not want to leave her hanging, wondering if you even bothered to call her friend. If the meeting ends up in business for you don't forget to send whatever reward to the referrer you give out for your referral program.

Testimonials

A testimonial is another form of Social Proof. Here you are asking for your customers to make a statement in written, verbal or video form telling others how much they like your product. This is made available from your website or other marketing media to corroborate to prospective customers the quality of your product and service.

You want your happy customers to tell their story. How you made them happy or solved a problem for them. It should not be an advertisement. You want people to hear and see the real customer, someone who looks and acts like them relating the benefits of your product simply and naturally.

You don't really want to pay for testimonials and many people shy away from even asking since they feel it is a conflict of interest to influence the commentary. However, you still need to ask, so at least ask your happiest customers. You may be pleasantly surprised at the amount of loyalty they have toward you.

Your evangelists will fall over backwards to help and the chance to be in a video is highly appealing to some people and a fate worse than death for others. Audio recordings can work as well.

This is a way to build up layers of marketing, getting your message out to people in many ways. Marketing requires multiple contacts to be effective, the more the better.

Social Media

The big buzzword in marketing is "social media." Social media encompasses Facebook, Twitter, LinkedIn, Pinterest, Google+, YouTube and dozens more. Business owners are told that it is necessary to use social media or you will be left behind unable to compete in the modern marketplace. In fact it is neither completely replacing traditional marketing nor is it inconsequential. It is a tool just like any other marketing medium and it has a place in the marketing tool kit like all the other tools.

Proper use of social media requires time and effort. It can be done quite inexpensively but in order to be heard amongst all the other voices out there doing the same thing it is necessary to develop a voice that it loud enough and unique enough to be heard.

To use social media effectively involves finding the right one or two or three platforms that work for you and your business and concentrating on them. For example, Facebook may be effective for a consumer product but not necessarily for a business to business product. Your customers will help you decide. A product that is visual in nature and used mostly by women might be well-represented by Pinterest. A business to business company might make use of LinkedIn.

Working with social media requires being present in the online community on the platform of choice. Look for posts by others, ones who have followers and make replies to their posts or comments to their blogs (thoughtful posts – not negative or impolite). Repost comments to your followers as well. Social media is about getting people to familiarize themselves with you and if you start by reposting others they will do the same for you.

If all do with social media is to send out advertising messages (and on some platforms that is not acceptable) you will end up pretty much being ignored. What you are doing is marketing not selling anyway. You want people to hear about you, to get a positive feeling about you and to become curious enough to want to get to know you and your product better.

This is a process of building your brand. The goal of Marketing is to touch people in as many ways, in as many forms as you can. You do not want every touch to be a sales contact or you will turn people off.

The Internet started out as a "free" medium and there are people who dislike any commercial use of it. This means that you need to know your audience to make sure your marketing messages are OK. Canada's Anti-Spam laws are such that you cannot solicit someone without having their permission before you send out your message. The U.S. laws are different and a bit more lenient but you cannot just send out whatever you want whenever you want to whomever you want anymore.

What you want to achieve is to get your potential customers paying attention to you and your posts, your content and to be drawn to your website. Part of this is to optimize your website so the people you want to talk to are drawn to it.

SEO

Search engine optimization (SEO) is Internet-speak for setting up your website so that when people who should be interested in your product are looking online and searching for it they end up finding it right at their fingertips.

This is done by putting keywords that are relevant to your business and your product into your blogs and into your web pages in such a way that the major search engines from Google, Bing, Yahoo and others find your website, others' references to your content and your other postings so that your site is displayed on the first page of search results.

Underneath the visible web pages there is what is called metadata – places to put information relevant to each web page that are also categorized by the search engines and used in determining how high you show up in the results pages of searches.

To track how well you are doing in web searches your website should be signed up with Google Analytics. It is a free service and you get analysis about how many and how often your website is visited: http://analytics.google.com/

I won't go into more detail on this subject as there is a huge amount of information available written by people much more knowledgeable than I.

Content Marketing

Asking people to buy products is rather problematical on the Internet. There are so many scammers out there, there is so much hyperbole, so many people selling stuff both good and bad. Many people do not respond as well as they may have in the past to the standard email sales pitch. Anti-spam laws now have teeth and limit your ability to solicit people without consent. Instead a different way of presenting yourself has arisen on the internet.

In a manner reminiscent of the seller in the marketplace displaying their wares for people to look over, many businesses are using their websites to allow people to look at their products for free, even to be able to download them as useable products without further obligation.

This is called Content Marketing and it is a way to earn credibility with your potential customers. By making information available in the form of Blogs, downloadable files and videos a company generates interest in its products. The content has to be of value – not just a Cracker Jack® box prize of little use – or it may backfire. You want people to be impressed with your content so they want to pay for more.

This content is presented without a sales pitch or with a minimal one. You might write a monthly, weekly or even a daily blog. You might have parts of your book or service available for download or you might have a video of your training class on your website for viewing. This content may be all that a web surfer is looking for and you may never hear from them again.

That's OK. Many of these lookie-loos would never be your customer in any event. You have touched them though and, who knows? At some point in the future they may hear about you from some other marketing touch point and you could still close the sale.

On the other hand you are hoping that your content will intrigue a passerby on the internet who will sign up for your newsletter or for a quote for your services. Once they see that your product is worthwhile then you can guide them into a position where you can close the sale.

Some thought has to go into the content you are providing since you don't want to give away the whole farm – eventually you want to sell something to your customers. It takes time and energy to create whatever intellectual property you are providing whether it is for free or for a fee. In your zeal to get the word out about your product you may create a situation where you have nothing to sell.

So be careful about the extent of your largesse. Keep the best to yourself. Give out the fluff but make sure it's quality fluff. Keep the core that requires thought and expertise and training to actualize.

Beguile your potential prospective customers with your understanding and knowledge and ability to communicate to them. There will be those who feel they must learn more from you and are willing to pay you for the privilege.

Email Marketing

Most online marketing is still done through email. In the past many web-based entrepreneurs have created or bought giant mail lists and send out messages over and over to the recipients, many of whom never see them. They end up in the Spam folder recognized for what they are. Even if they make it into the inbox most of them are never opened.

I've mentioned the CASL – Canadian Anti-Spam Legislation several times in this book. As of this writing, it has just taken effect and it requires that thoughtless spamming cease. This is actually an opportunity in disguise. Instead of sending out unread messages to many, many people you should be talking to a much smaller target audience. Since you have to ask permission to send emails before they are sent you will only be sending them to people who might actually open up your messages.

This is a much better opportunity. Rather than trying to manage an unwieldy list full of inactive addresses and unwilling recipients you get a targeted message that can be much more specific and have much greater impact on your prospective customers.

Traditional Media

Newspaper and magazine display ads, billboards, flyers and door hangers, TV and Radio are all traditional media. As we have discussed this is characterized by the concept of interruption and repetition. You interrupt what people are doing to get their hopefully undivided attention. This may be accomplished through the color of an ad, the headline, music, noise, movement, etc.

Traditional media is called mass-marketing because it is indiscriminate. You touch everybody in the hope of reaching a few people who are actually interested in your product. Because of the necessity to be repetitive it becomes more annoying than interesting especially for those who are not potential customers.

There may be a place for traditional media in your marketing activities depending on your business. Be careful of listening to the hype you may hear about the ability to reach you target demographic though coverage during the time your demographic is actively listening to that station.

Often radio and TV salespersons will "throw in" their off-hours ads for a seemingly small increase in price. Realize that although they will tell you otherwise they are unloading unpopular times that that nobody else is willing to pay for. This it their method of bundling products to increase their profits while filling undesirable commercial slots.

A good radio ad campaign will have repetitive ads at the same time every day in drive time spots and it will cost you thousands of dollars per month to be effective. You also need to run these ads for long periods of time not a few days or weeks.

Display ads in the newspaper have been declining in value to the entrepreneur. They just don't get the results they may have in the past because of the decline in newspaper readership and the competition from all the other ad sources out there. The same with inserts in the paper. These are usually call-to-action ads. They will have a coupon or a sale or some reason why the potential customer needs to buy now.

> Handyman Joe has done most of his prospecting by sending out flyers to specific postal walks in the area he works in. If he sends out 20,000 flyers he knows that he will generate about 100 phone calls from prospective customers – a 0.5% response rate. Of those 100 prospective customers 50 end up signing up with him to do a job which earns him an average of $500 in revenues each.

> This means since it costs Joe about 2¢ per flyer to print and 11¢ to mail it costs him $2,600 and therefore he spends $52 to generate a new customer.

> A problem with these types of ads is that you are in some fashion or another offering discounts. Although you really want to avoid reducing your price you still need a call to action to get a response before it slips away from the mind of the recipient. We will explore this in Chapter 7 when we talk about Customer Service.

If Joe is able to increase the number of Prospective customers through his marketing efforts what happens to his profits? In the examples used in this book Joe is making small changes. These small changes end up resulting in large results. Small changes are also much easier to attain than expecting large wholesale turnarounds.

	Start	Add 10% Prospects
Prospects	2,000	2,200
Conversion Rate	50%	50%
# of Customers	1,000	1,100
Price	$500	$500
Repeat Customers	1.0	1.0
Total Revenues	$500,000	$550,000
Profit Margin	6.0%	8.4%
Profits	$30,000	$46,000

Figure 14. Increase Prospects by 10%

Joint Ventures & Affiliates – The One-Stop-Shop

As you do networking and talk to people while trying to build up your business you will start meeting others who don't necessarily need your product but who are in areas that are complementary to yours. Even competitors might be worthwhile keeping in your virtual Rolodex.

The reason is that there will be times when you are not the right business for this customer. It may be that your customer has mentioned needs that are outside your area of expertise. It may be that she is outside your geographical area or that you know someone with better skills than you. Perhaps you are out of your product or unavailable to perform the service when the customer wants it.

Rather than sending the customer away when you cannot help her refer the customer to someone you know. You may have a formal affiliate referral arrangement where you get paid $50 or a percentage of the proceeds for the referral. You may be affiliated with the other person informally or you may not even know each other at all. The better you know the person you are making the referral to the better since your reputation can be affected by the quality of the work you your affiliate does for your customer.

The One-Stop Shop is where you avoid sending prospective customers away without finding a solution to their problem. You want them to get in the habit of calling you whenever they have an issue you might be able to help them with even if they don't know if you can do the work.

> Handyman Joe built up a list of other businesses he could call to refer business to when he couldn't do the job or it was out of his area of expertise. When a customer called and he was not able to do the job they asked or if the job he was doing for them involved bringing in others he had a list of people he could go to.
>
> He was determined that he would never send off a prospective customer without finding her a referral of some kind. He did not like just telling people to go look up names in the phone book. He would even look up names himself in the phone book or in the Better Business Bureau website if he had to.
>
> What he did was to create a One-Stop-shop for his customers. He trained them to call him for any home repair need not just things he normally did. It cost his

office a little extra time and effort but the extra loyalty he got from his customers more than paid for his efforts.

By setting up affiliate relationships he now had a network of people feeding him back another source of prospective customers that he could convert into customers. He also made his customers happy that he could help them out when they did not know who to call as well.

With some affiliates he was even able to set up appointments directly on behalf of his customers. This way he made sure the customer reached the right person and was helped properly.

He checked up on his customers after the work was done the same as if he had done the work himself. This served to further cement his relationship with his customers while allowing him to evaluate the quality of his referral sources.

Establishing Joint Ventures or Affiliate partnerships with natural partners working together with you is a big benefit for you and your business. If you own a wine store wouldn't it make sense to have a go-to partner who sells cheeses or picnic baskets? If you are a carpenter it helps to affiliate with plumbers, tile setters and electricians of course but how about pest control companies, asbestos and mold abatement companies and insurance companies doing restoration work?

It's the follow-up process that makes this work. Don't just send your prospect off into the wild without making sure they have a solution that you created for them. If one solution does not work try another.

The Affiliate Call Process:

- Mrs. Smith calls up with a request for your product you cannot handle - you have an affiliate or a joint venture arrangement with someone who can help her.

- Tell Mrs. Smith about his experience and capability to help her.

- Ask Mrs. Smith when she can meet with him and if you can make an appointment on her behalf. You can even do this while she is on the phone or in your store.

- You call up the affiliate and tell him that you are sending Mrs. Smith over to him. Tell him that you know how well they will take care of Mrs. Smith.

- Ask to make an appointment for Mrs. Smith now. Verify the appointment with Mrs. Smith.

- Follow up with the affiliate and Mrs. Smith both to to make sure they are both satisfied.

- Send them each a handwritten Thank-You note.

- You have just strengthened your relationship with both Mrs. Smith and your affiliate.

Figure 15. The Affiliate Call Process

Chapter 5

Conversion Rate – Sales

Conversion of Prospective Customers into Customers is the province of the Salesman. Many people hate the idea of sales and selling as it has gotten a really bad rap over the years and for good reason. As the word cloud for adjectives for the word "Sales" (Pink, 2012) shows the high-pressure used-car salesman, obnoxious TV and Radio marketing and internet spam have left people feeling manipulated and have caused the public to lose faith that businesses are capable of ethical operation.

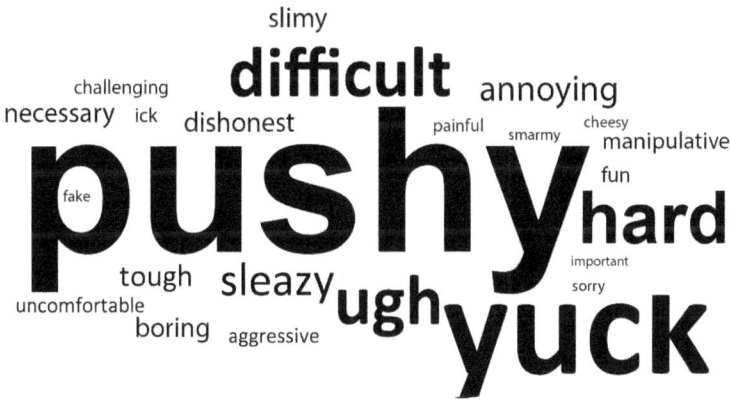

slimy
challenging **difficult** annoying
necessary ick dishonest painful smarmy cheesy manipulative
fake **pushy** fun **hard**
tough sleazy important
uncomfortable **ugh** sorry
boring aggressive **yuck**

Figure 16. Word Cloud for "Sales" Adjectives

Business scandals over the years about Enron, the Internet Bubble, the Banking Crisis, Tyco and Bernie Madoff's Ponzi scheme have all created fear of business and the feeling that business ethics is an oxymoron.

Yet you are not going to be able to sell your products without some form of salesmanship being involved. The idea that you make a better mousetrap and the world will beat a path to your door is a fine idea but in practice that is not how it works. You still have to generate prospective customers and you still have to convert those prospects into customers and that is the province of Sales.

The ratio of customers to prospects is called the Conversion Rate. You can calculate the Conversion Rate by dividing the number of Customers you have by the number of Prospective Customers in your Sales Funnel.

Figure 17. Conversion Rate

People buy because they trust what you are saying about your product. The closer this number gets to 100% the better you are at establishing trust and converting Prospects into Customers.

Does anybody feel comfortable going into a car dealership to buy a car? Customers are taken in by slick, manipulative salesmen who seem to hold all the cards in the deal leaving her feeling that she has vastly overpaid. Buyer's Remorse sets in immediately after signing the contract.

If you think about it though, sales is actually part of life. When you go out on a date, aren't you selling yourself? Be honest here. Haven't you taken extra care to clean up, wear nice clothes, and put on your best behaviour all just to sell ourselves to your date?

So, in sales as on a date, think about what you want to accomplish. What is your ultimate goal? You want to sell the customer on the benefits of the product (whether it is your suitability as a potential partner or a family car). You want to create legitimate interest within your prospective customer for your product without overselling or being disingenuous.

Ultimately, You Must Ask for the Order

Many salespersons feel that if they just have the right words or pitch the prospect will fall into their lap and say yes without thinking. You can certainly ruin a deal by saying the <u>wrong</u> thing but in reality sincerity and polite persistence are the keys to closing the deal because that is the pathway to a trusting relationship.

You want to set the stage for success when selling. Building rapport and trust is a must. If you can achieve that then you will make the sale. So, how do you go about building trust? If you are selling a retail product beyond having a superlative product you need to have well-trained and knowledgeable staff, a well-stocked and welcoming store and a generous return policy.

How do you make your own buying decisions? Do you spend a lot of time looking at each and every choice? Or are all of your purchases impulse buys? In reality the answer usually is, "It depends". We may want to feel that we are pretty rational about our purchases but there are many biases and unconscious factors that shape our decisions. But think about what major things influence you.

> I was in a department store recently looking for a new sofa. Time was a bit short but I was determined I would find one and buy it then and there. I had a couple of sofas in mind from a sales brochure but was open to some ideas.

The salesman was on the phone most of the time I was there and I felt that he really didn't have his heart in the sale. In the end even though I had actually had him write up the purchase I ultimately decided not to go through with it.

Why not? Partly it was due to the sales process. The salesman was distracted by his phone and had other customers he was trying to help at the same time so was unable to give me his undivided attention.

When he did talk to me he kept upselling me – trying to get me interested in buying a sofa at a higher price than I told him I was willing to pay – and when he was ringing up the order all of a sudden there were a lot of unexpected extra charges.

In spite of the higher price of the sofa I agreed to buy it at first but then after a few moments I abruptly cancelled the sale. The final straw wasn't that there was an extra cost for delivery, it was that the costs were higher than expected and they came across as deceptively hidden charges.

When I thought about it I realized it was not really the cost so much as his attitude and his level of service that turned me off to the sale. I told him what I wanted and he kept showing me sofas that were out of my price range and just hadn't listened to my needs.

Showing respect for your customer is important. For example, I never take calls when I meet with someone. If I know I really need to take a call I try to explain it in advance. I have had clients themselves get quite antsy when my phone rings and I won't answer it even though I tell them it's OK that it goes into voicemail.

But what is the message you send to customers if you take a phone call when they are sitting right in front of you? It is that they are less important than somebody who is jumping the queue and interrupting with a more urgent communication.

Is more urgent more important? Normally the person who has taken the time to make an appointment and come to see me personally should be considered the priority. That is what voicemail is for anyway. Very few phone calls are that urgent that they cannot be returned at a later time.

Avoid the tyranny of the urgent over the important. If you are trying to move a prospect along the buying path don't sabotage your efforts by showing her disrespect. Sometimes things do happen and you have to deal with them immediately. Most people understand this. The fact that you are busy is an indication that your work is good since you would not be working if you did not have satisfied customers.

You get some leeway with customers and prospects but if you continually fail to show on time or keep taking phone calls or make mistakes with your service you have created a liability for yourself instead of a satisfied customer.

USP – Unique Selling Proposition

What is special about your product? Why should I buy from you instead of anybody else? Why should I care? When you can answer those questions you have your unique selling proposition usually in the form of a one-line statement. This is both a marketing and a sales tool.

Your USP helps you to focus and define your brand. It is your way of communicating the value of your product to your prospective customers in a succinct fashion. Keep your USP in mind when writing ad copy. Keep your USP in mind when you are working at developing your product. Use it in your sales pitch.

The USP connects you with your customer base. It is the essence of your business in a nutshell. In a few words it tells people why they should buy from you and not from your competition.

Famous USPs

FEDEX – When it absolutely, positively has to be there overnight

Mercedes-Benz – The best-engineered car in the world

DeBeers – A diamond is forever.

M&Ms – The milk chocolate melts in your mouth, not in your hand.

Avis – We're number two. We try harder.

What is Your USP? _____

Sales Training

Anybody from your business who has any contact with a prospective customer or a customer in fact is a salesperson. Any person in your organization who touches a potential buyer can affect the future of your business. This includes you as the owner, your sales staff, your administration personnel, shipping staff, your after-sales service and support and your repair persons. Customer service training is essential for any of these people.

We will discuss this more in Chapter 7, Repeat Business

As we have discussed before, to get to <u>YES</u> you need to establish trust between yourself and your potential customer. It is a personal bond even if it is through your website. Think about those times when you felt really comfortable or happy about handing your money over to a business when the work was complete.

There was a personal connection of some kind. You were made comfortable, your immediate needs looked after. Perhaps the salesperson chatted with you a bit about something personal that you shared. You were put at ease. The benefits of the product to you were brought up and the advantages that would accrue to you discussed.

Your questions were answered and a sense of urgency to buy was there but not the focus. The cost was not the focus. The salesman's interest was not the focus.

A high quality product backed by a sense of trust in the seller sells itself. All you have to do then is ask for the order. If you've done it very well sometimes the customer will even demand to buy before you can ask the question.

How do you generate that demand? By practicing extreme customer service. See the Customer Sales Process Map. Be deliberate in mapping your buying process as this will help you track your customer conversions better. Knowing what you are doing and where you can improve can make a big difference to your conversion rate without costing you any extra money.

<u>Customer Sales Process Map</u>

- Understand your customers' needs
    - Find out what their needs are:
        - Surveys
        - Online forms
        - Talking to them

- Focus on the customer and build the relationship. Put yourself in his shoes and turn it into a buying rather than a selling process.
- Ask lots of questions. This will help you to qualify your customers, find out what they need and if you can genuinely offer them something of value.
- Add some authority and credibility to what you offer by providing detailed customer testimonials.
- Schedule several follow ups with prospects and each time you contact them provide them with useful information.
- Give customers a reason to buy now, offer added value or special limited offers as incentives.

Figure 18. Customer Sales Process Map

Risk Reversal

On the Internet "risk reversal" is jargon for "guarantee." No matter what you call it your prospect needs to know that if she has a problem with your product you will take care of it quickly and simply. Knowing that the risk she takes purchasing your product has been reduced it is much easier for her trust you enough to to say "yes" when you ask for the order.

The interesting thing is that many people will not take advantage of a guarantee even if it is clearly in their best interest to do so. Normally, you can expect 1-2% refund requests from customers. Knowing that you have the confidence in your product to offer the guarantee makes it easier for your prospective customers to believe in you and your product.

If you think about it you really have a guarantee anyway. If a customer were to call you up and say he is dissatisfied with your product it is unlikely you will just turn him away telling him that it's not your problem. So formalize your guarantee and publicize it. Make it an unconditional guarantee and reduce the perceived risk to the prospect.

Abiding by your guarantee is just as important as having one in the first place. Do you think that quibbling over whether a customer has the right to a refund will be a positive for your business? Is it more important to be right or to keep a great reputation intact? Reading the fine print to a customer categorizes you as a bean counter not a practitioner of extreme customer service.

There are times when you need to defend your business against unethical customers but much more often you need to just move on and learn how to do it better the next time. I have always felt that putting in lots of conditions for coupons puts a barrier between my customers and me. Write your ad copy clearly in the first place rather than trying to ferret out the few customers who will try to take advantage of you.

As consumers ourselves, we put up with a lot of bad customer service from businesses of all sizes every day. A potential opportunity to enhance customer loyalty is squandered when businesses ignore customer concerns. Your iron-clad, no-risk, money back-if-not-100% satisfied guarantee can generate incredible customer loyalty when you turn a negative customer experience into a positive one.

Follow-up support is part of Chapter 7, Repeat Customers and we will explore it more there.

The Sale

The principles of selling are not new. Any book by Napoleon Hill, Dale Carnegie or Zig Ziglar gives you the rudiments of selling. Newer authors build upon the originals and give you a modern take on mastery of the art and science of persuasion. See my list of Recommended Books at the end of the book for a short list of many readings on sales, selling and persuasion.

The key to closing the sale is to be polite and to be persistent in order to establish a trusting relationship with the prospective customer. Once trust is established you can ask for the order.

It is important to establish an environment where the customer can feel comfortable with your communications. It helps to have a "reason to call." If you don't have some level of trust established you are making cold calls and a cold call can be very difficult to make.

A cold call is where you are trying to get interest in your product from people who don't know you, don't know about you, don't care about your or your product and don't really want you to waste their time. Many people have earned a living this way as many people have but it is pretty brutal and not for those easily discouraged.

Is The Extrovert Really The Best Salesperson?

Many people think that the most successful salesperson is someone who is very gregarious, very outgoing – the extravert.

Pink (Pink, 2012, p. 82) quotes a study that claims that the more extraverted you are the LESS likely you are able to close a sale. In fact the extreme extraverts are not much better at selling than extreme introverts.

The case of the introverted salesperson is pretty obvious. The introvert spends so much time listening that he can't ask for the order. However, while the extravert, is better able to connect with people, tends to talk so much that she forgets to stop talking and spend time listening to the customer.

Sales Revenues by Extraversion Level

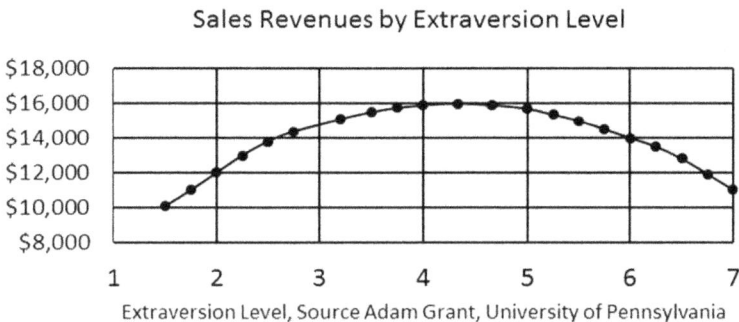

Extraversion Level, Source Adam Grant, University of Pennsylvania

Figure 19. Sales by Level of Extraversion

The moral is, if you are introverted you need to communicate more, ask more questions and ask for the order. If you are extraverted you need to stop talking, listen to the prospective customer, ask more questions and don't forget to ask for the order.

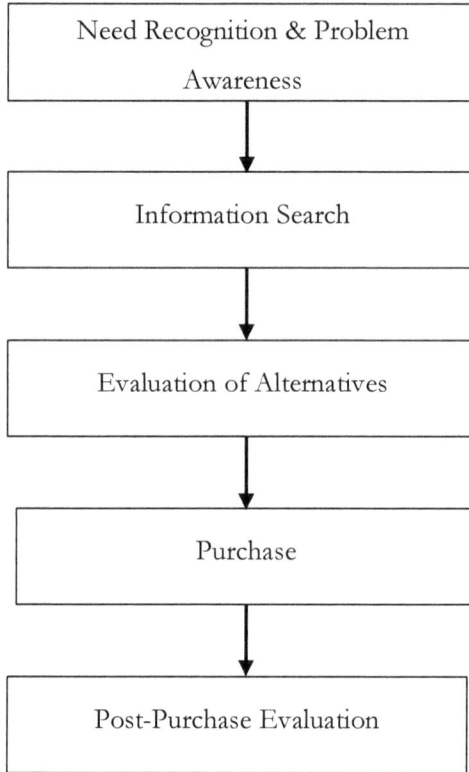

```
┌─────────────────────────────────┐
│   Need Recognition & Problem     │
│           Awareness              │
└─────────────────────────────────┘
                 │
                 ▼
┌─────────────────────────────────┐
│       Information Search         │
└─────────────────────────────────┘
                 │
                 ▼
┌─────────────────────────────────┐
│     Evaluation of Alternatives   │
└─────────────────────────────────┘
                 │
                 ▼
┌─────────────────────────────────┐
│            Purchase              │
└─────────────────────────────────┘
                 │
                 ▼
┌─────────────────────────────────┐
│     Post-Purchase Evaluation     │
└─────────────────────────────────┘
```

Figure 20. The 5-Step Customer Buying Process

Persistence and the Customer Buying Process

It is necessary to understand the importance of repetition and persistence in marketing and sales. There is a five-step buying process customers go through. It takes time and the last salesperson they talk to is generally the one who gets the order.

It is not set in stone and customers start and exit at different points but the five-step buying process gives you an idea of how we, as customers, determine which products are the products we buy. If you provide for these steps with your prospects you can control the deal from start to finish and you are likely to close more sales.

Sometimes the customer is gathering information and the salesperson may not feel it is worth giving her the time of day because she appears to be "just looking" with no real purchasing decision point in sight.

The smart salesperson recognizes that if she starts the trust-creation process now the customer is much more likely to return there than to go with the person who just ignores them or treats them poorly

Think about those times when you may have been gathering information about a product and either physically gone into various stores and talked to salespersons or browsed different websites. Were you impressed enough to come back even if you went somewhere else to keep getting information? Or were you pressured to buy? Were you just plain ignored or were you asked if you wanted help?

Did you know that 67% of all internet shopping baskets are left unpurchased? (Macdonald, 2012) Why? (WorldPay.com, 2012, p. 16) said that 56% of prospects left the website without buying because they were presented with unexpected costs and 26% thought the site was too difficult to navigate.

However, the merchants themselves thought that declined credit cards was the main reason for cart abandonment. (it was the least concern for consumers). It is obvious that customers want value and ease of transaction process.

To stem this tide online businesses are using pop-up messages leading you back to the checkout, follow-up emails offering discounts – in fact some purchasers are now expecting the offer of a discount and wait for the discount offer before they commit to the purchase.

Frequency of Contact

Even experienced salespersons fail to follow up with their prospective customers. It takes at least 4 contacts for most sales to occur. Yet many salespersons won't even make a 2nd attempt.

A prospect may be making his first foray looking into this particular product or service or it may be her 6th. When the buying decision is made you want to be the one who is in front of the customer at the time the customer makes his final decision. Often, people won't return on their own.

Salesperson Follow-ups	Contacts Per Sale
• 48% NEVER follow up	• 2% on the 1st contact
• 25% make 2 contacts	• 3% on the 2nd contact
• 12% make 3 contacts	• 5% on the 3rd contact
• 10% make 4 or more contacts	• 10% on the 4th contact
	• 80% of all closings are made on the 5th – the 12th contact

Figure 21. Salesman Follow-Ups with Contacts

Balance of Power

In the days before the internet the salesman had the upper hand. The reason was that the salesman had all the information about the product. If you were buying a car where did you get information about the manufacturing cost? Kelley Blue Book, a book put out by an independent organization was pretty much the only source. If you were lucky you could find an out-of-date copy in your local library.

In the movie, Glengarry, Glen Ross, based on David Mamet's play of the same name (Mamet, 1992), Alec Baldwin plays a successful alpha-male salesman who meets with a group of less than stellar compatriots and in no uncertain terms tells them what it truly takes to be salesmen in his world.

Unfortunately, these are the old-style smarmy type salesmen. They are selling real-estate in Florida that were located far from where they were being sold. The lots were far enough away that nobody would have been able to see them. In reality, they were underwater or unbuildable sites worth far less than they were being sold for if they even existed at all.

In the play the salesmen could be seen pressuring prospective customers to meet with them so they could sell them this property. Their tactic was to talk so quickly, so eloquently and so forcefully that they essentially bullied people into buying their products. They created an illusion of trust, the same way the old-style used-car salesman would fabricate or embellish information that would lead a customer to buy whether they wanted or needed this product or not.

Often afterward the customer had "Buyer's Remorse." This is a term meaning that after the purchase, after the luster of the deal had worn off, the customer was left with a feeling that the value received for the product was much lower than the money paid for it. This is why generating a false trust is not the way to generate repeat business or referrals.

In the Internet Age of today many people have started doing their research often exclusively online. In a practice called "Showrooming," shoppers will physically visit department or big box stores to determine if the product is what they want then go online to find the best source rather than buy if from the store.

This consumer behavior is considered unethical by businesses and many stores have gone to great lengths to stop it – to the extent of banning such shoppers or charging them a shopping fee. Of course this is counterproductive as it creates bad negative buzz for the company.

A better way to battle this phenomenon is to create a more attractive environment to prevent the customer from leaving the store, offer price incentives, free delivery, fast delivery/availability and more.

With the ability to shop online and learn more about the product than the salesperson the balance of power has shifted to the buyer. Now the salesperson cannot just obfuscate and withhold the truth from the savvy shopper. He has to be part of the shopper's solution, to provide higher levels of customer service and support instead.

Call Reluctance

Many of the books and seminars on sales produced over the years involve ways to get over "call reluctance," the fear of calling or contacting prospective customers. Even the best of salespersons get this feeling at some point or another in their careers. When you are selling anything, whether it is an idea to the boss, a new product to prospective customers or your business to prospective investors call reluctance can be a factor you must overcome.

Call reluctance is manifested by procrastination. You start to put off making calls or setting up meetings or sending emails to prospective customers. This process takes longer and longer to start each day. Eventually you are just sitting there doing anything except the activities you know you need to do to bring in customers and money for your business.

This can be a result of hearing "No" so many times that you develop an aversion to anything that might elicit that word. Since the commissioned salesperson's entire livelihood depends on the ability to overcome this problem there are many ways to deal with it.

One way is to set up a competition with a fellow salesperson. Set goals and whoever reaches the goal first wins and the other has to buy lunch. The goal can be number of attempts or it can be number of "yeses" ore even counting "no's." Don't forget that it is the activities you want to concentrate on not the results.

Another way is to tally your attempts. Once you reach a certain number you can give yourself permission to perform a procrastinating activity such as web surfing for a short time or go buy a candy bar or get a cup of coffee. Some salespersons put a nickel in a jar for every activity they perform until they reach a certain amount then use it to buy a reward.

For the most stubborn cases of call reluctance you put money into an envelope and address it to a cause you utterly abhor, and give it to a friend. She will mail it off if you do not reach your goal. It has to be a significant amount of money though. It could be a Conservative voter writing a check for $5,000 to the Green Party or a Democrat writing one out to the Republican Party. Now, what would that do for helping you overcome your call reluctance?

This is a Band-Aid approach though. It does not remove the problem itself. A different way to look at call reluctance is to consider it to be an issue of not having a good reason to call. If you are cold-calling you really do not have a reason to call the person on the other end of the phone line. This makes most people uncomfortable because they can see themselves on the receiving end and know how upset they would be to get such unsolicited communications themselves.

It is much easier to call someone if you know ahead of time that she will be happy to answer your call. This is what I mean by having a reason to call. How do you do this? First of all you need to have a list of people that you have already been in contact with who have given you permission.

When you are out networking and meeting people you need to be asking them for permission to contact them. With the anti-spam requirements in Canada you are not allowed to send an email asking for permission to contact them anyway. Permission has to be given in advance. When exchanging business cards ask for permission to contact him and send an email stating that you are asking to keep in touch based on your verbal communication of (date).

Using referrals properly is another way. Always make reference to the referrer when you contact a prospect referred to you. This lowers the barrier and makes it a warm call allowing you to more easily make contact. This is also why you may hear cold-callers ask you for referrals even if you don't know them. If they can get names from you it turns their next cold call into a warm call.

Sales Process

The classic sales process can be summed up by the acronym, AIDA (Communication Theory.org, 2010) (it was even mentioned in Glengarry, Glen Ross (Mamet, 1992) and it was

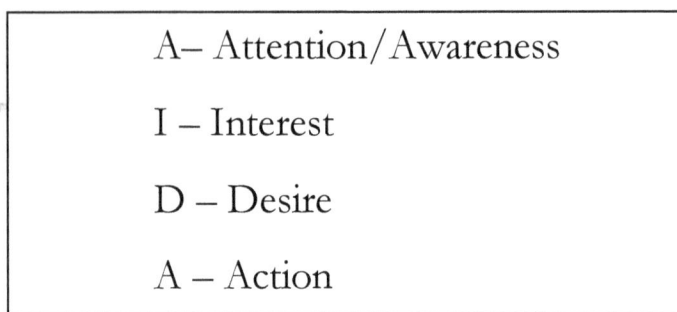

A– Attention/Awareness

I – Interest

D – Desire

A – Action

Figure 22. AIDA

initially devised in 1898 by E. St. Elmo Lewis. The sales funnel is a graphic representation of this concept.

Attention means to attract the attention of the customer. We see this all the time in TV advertising. Interest means to raise customer interest by focusing on benefits instead of features. Desire means to elicit desire in the customer for the product. Action is the call to action or to ask for the order so the customer actually buys the product.

AIDA is still useful today but there are many more modern versions based on the psychological studies of sales and selling and we will look at one of them instead.

A more modern version of AIDA is ADOCA (Grethel, 2011). There are many ways to present the sales process but they all involve the five steps outlined here. Some people break the process down into 7 or 10 steps. The main thing is using polite persistence and asking questions to learn the customers' needs and wants.

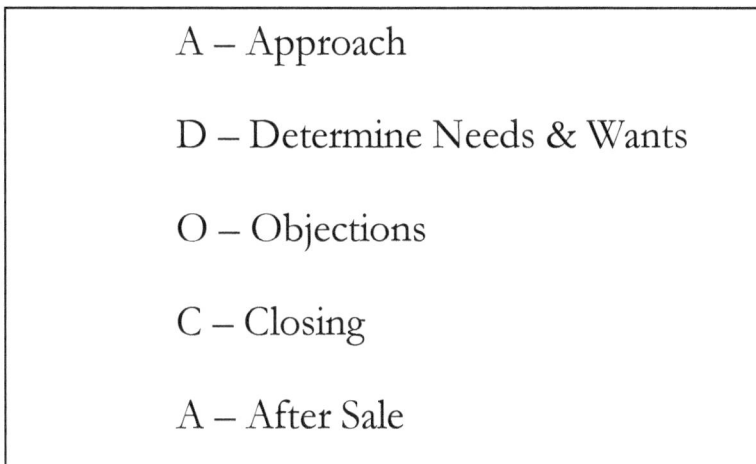

A – Approach

D – Determine Needs & Wants

O – Objections

C – Closing

A – After Sale

Figure 23. ADOCA

Approach

Approaching the customer is the way you generate some interest from the shopper to make her want to learn more and to want to move closer to purchasing your product. Marketing awareness generates interest and the customer is moved to learn more. At this point the customer may be ready to buy or not.

If your customer is ready to buy she may skip the next step or may jump right into it. Everybody is different. If it is a car or a house there may be a prolonged period of searching and comparing. If it is a candy bar it may just be an impulse purchase and the search ends then and there. In a retail store the customer enters and the staff is usually trained to make some kind of contact.

Even before you approach your customer there is legwork you want to have accomplished. Qualify your prospect, find out if she is interested and have the means and desire to purchase it. Make sure you have all the contact information correct such as phone numbers and email addresses, spellings and pronunciations.

Determine Needs and Wants

The way to figure out what the customer needs is to ask questions. Good questioning technique is key to the ability to generate trust and to make sure what the customer is offered and what he gets is what he needs. Sometimes customers don't really know what they want or need. Sometimes customers don't even know how your product can be of value to them.

A really good sales clerk will first try to engage a potential customer in a friendly manner, trying to read from her what she wants and what her personality style is. If rebuffed the clerk may try a different tack, perhaps asking about color taste or if the customer is shopping for herself or someone else.

If done in a modest way it is not offensive to the non-shopper such as myself and it is enticing to the person like my partner who expects sales help. By sidling up to the issue it is possible to get a chance to engage the customer without pressing her.

Find out what she wants when she walks into your store, opens your website or has a coffee meeting with you. Why is he there? Is she serious? Is he "kicking tires?" When would she be ready to buy?

Test out different approaches with different people and jot down the results. Do people respond to a very brash come-on? Do they respond to a compliment or a positive comment? Everybody is different and responds differently even the same person at different times.

It is much easier to be grow your business if you have a scripted process to manage customers. Suppose you <u>are</u> very good at handling sales. What happens when you grow enough to hire another salesperson? How will you transfer your knowledge and skill to this new person? Will you leave it to chance? Or will you just expect them to be as good as you?

Objections

Often a customer will respond to a sales pitch with an objection. "It's too expensive." "I don't need it." "It is too inconvenient." "I need to talk to my spouse first." The salesperson needs to be able to answer those concerns and many others. After a few times talking to customers the major objections for your product will come to light and you should be prepared to answer them.

At this point the ability to politely and persistently answer those concerns is the key to ending up at yes. Selling on the internet is more complex because if a visitor is not engaged quickly, if he does not feel compelled to learn more and to investigate the answers to his questions he will move on and you will never even know he was there.

On the Internet you do not have the luxury to deal with prospects individually and you must have all questions answered in advance and easily found on your website.

Risk reversal is even more important with online sales. By making sure the potential customer is comfortable that you will make good on concerns about a long-distance purchase you have taken away one of the biggest objections they will have. If I know that I have recourse in case of product failure then it is much easier for me to trust you and the barriers to purchase lower.

The first step in managing objections is to first take them seriously. In our nervousness or fear of dealing with objections

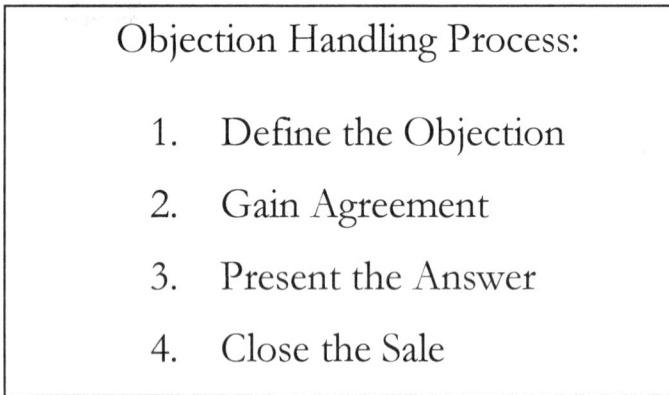

Objection Handling Process:

1. Define the Objection

2. Gain Agreement

3. Present the Answer

4. Close the Sale

Figure 24. Handling Objections

often those concerns are just ignored or glossed over. Repeat the objection back to the customer and ask questions to make sure you understand what it is. Sometimes raising an objection is a customer's way of avoiding telling you, "no." In order to deal with it you need to know what the problem actually is.

After listening to the prospect, ask probing questions and clarify your understanding then repeat it back to the customer to make sure you are in agreement on the issue.

For example, is the customer's concern really about the price? When asking about details you may find that it is the customer's ability to pay full price right now that is the issue. Perhaps you could give her the opportunity to defer payment or pay in installments.

Perhaps a competitor has a lower price. You need to be able to tell her what features and benefits of your product make it worth the higher price.

You want to gain agreement that you understand the issue and that it is the only issue – that there are not others lurking about. The first issue is often not the most important. People tend to defer discussing things that are truly dear to them and unless you have real trust you may not be privy to their innermost concerns.

If it is about time reassure him that you have the ability (truthfully) to get the job done on time or if not you tell him what you <u>can</u> do. If it is about trust tell her about your guarantee and show her testimonials and other social proof you are who you say you are and that you will do what you say you do.

This is where the written contract is important for any work or project that may end up with any kind of ambiguity. The contract is to protect both you and the customer.

> In Handyman Joe's business very few of his competitors use contracts. Quite often he would hear stories from his customers about disastrous misunderstandings that occurred due to verbal contracts. Written contracts help because if they are written properly they clearly outline the project scope. A written contract is much more easily

enforceable in the event of a misunderstanding, especially if it ends up in court.

A written contract is a good way to make sure that all concerns are addressed up front. It becomes part of the guarantee since it limits the scope of work while making sure nothing is forgotten.

The Close

At some point you have to ask for the order. It can be as straightforward as simply asking the customer to buy your product or it can be a more subtle approach. In some fashion it is necessary to lead the customer into taking action. In fact if you don't ask you even may even upset some prospective customers who feel that you are disrespecting them. They may even get up and leave from frustration.

Many salespersons, especially entrepreneurs, feel that having to ask the customer for their money is beneath them. If a potential customer likes their product so much why would they have to ask? The reason is that many people will sit on the fence even if they know the product is in their best interest to purchase. They will avoid having to make a decision and avoid taking out their wallet to consummate the deal. You need to help those people get over their inertia.

Sometimes you reach an impasse. The customer may just not be ready to buy but has not said an outright no. At this point you may need to defer the decision with the customer until she is ready to buy.

Learning to Take Yes for an Answer

Sometimes a salesperson gets so wrapped up in his pitch that even when the buying signs are present he is either so unself-confident or unaware of his audience that he fails to see that the prospect is ready to buy. He feels that he must make sure that he gets all the information out on the table and cannot stop his pitch.

At this point his prospect is getting impatient and is either sitting politely, nodding her head and looking at her watch or worse, is getting ready to get up and leave. This is The Salesperson Who Won't Take Yes For An Answer. Pay attention to the prospect and watch body language, listen for questions and look for the Yes. Extroverts are prone to this problem as they get wrapped up in their spiel rather than attend to the customer.

> While in negotiations with a very experienced salesperson I had already decided that I would purchase his product. However he was determined to shoulder on with his pitch when I was actually just asking questions for clarification and understanding of the contract not raising objections.
>
> I had already told him I was going to buy his product and he still would not "take Yes for an answer". He had to get through his whole presentation and even became quite antagonistic with me because he thought I was not listening to him.
>
> I found myself telling him to stop selling me but he still could not stop himself. I bought the product anyway but it was not in any way due to his sales expertise or closing ability. On the contrary the only reason he didn't lose the order was that his product was unique and I needed it for my project.

How do you know that a customer wants to buy your product? The first way is for you to ask. If he says "Yes," guess what? He is ready to buy. I know this is a glib statement but it's OK to take Yes for an answer. Ring up the sale and wrap up the product. Your job is done If you keep talking you may end up un-selling the product and lose the sale.

Buying signs are indications, sometimes unconscious, that the customer is in agreement with you and is feeling positive about your product. At this point he may be ready to buy or maybe not. This is where you go for the trial close.

An example would be after you answer an objection. You can ask, "Have I answered all of your questions? How about we ring up the sale?" Or "We take cash and major credit cards. How would you like to pay?" Or "I can have the product delivered to you tomorrow. What is your address?"

At this point the customer will say either Yes, No or Maybe. If she says yes, complete the sale. If she says no arrange for a time to call her back or get in touch with her when she is ready. Ask if she has any concerns you haven't answered. If there are concerns go back to your objection handling process and ask for the order again. If you hear a maybe, try to find out what her concern is, answer it and ask for the order again.

If all else fails, it is time to let her go or, better yet tell her that you will give her a follow-up call in a few days or a week or a month. Many times customers will tell you they will call you and you should counter with your promise to call – and then make the call.

You now have a reason to call – you promised her you would call and now you make good on your promise. Do not let the customer take control here as few people will make those return calls – even people who actually intend on calling back will get busy and forget.

After Sale Support

After sale support cements the relationship and encourages your customers to turn into evangelists for you and for your business. This is the part that also gets the most neglect from the entrepreneur. In fact many business owners feel that if they contact the customer after the sale they are "bugging them."

How would you feel though if you received a hand-written thank-you card from a store owner thanking you for your business? Would you feel more positive toward the business or less? What if there was an encouragement to come back – a coupon for the next purchase or a request for referrals? Would you reject that? We will discuss this subject more in Ch. 7, Repeat Customers.

You Can Turn Dislike into Like When You Ask For a Favor

A story from Benjamin Franklin's days relates how he turned an active enemy into a friend by asking to borrow a rare book from his library then sending him a thank-you note. (You Are Not So Smart, 2011)

This runs contrary to what you might expect but it is innate in us humans to feel more kindly toward someone who has the good taste and good sense to know that we are the best person around for that task.

If you have a less than happy customer, ask her to do something for you. Perhaps fill out a questionnaire. Perhaps come into the store to return the product. In any event you want to blunt the negativity. Bending over backwards is not always enough and can compromise your principles.

Make sure you have a way of contacting customers. Ask for permission to send them some information from time to time assuring them you will not just send advertising. Send your customers useful and valuable information. This is a method to remain at TOMA with your customers.

Handyman Joe Learns How to Sell

Handyman Joe realized that his craftsmen were a major part of his sales staff but they were not always the best representatives of his organization. This is a group of people who act as solopreneurs without any kind of sales training excepting what they had picked up on their own.

Because the calls he received were from people already wanting his services he knew they were already partway along the sales path. Yet he was only winning half the bids his contractors responded to.

When he analyzed his financial results he realized that there were opportunities to improve his conversion rate. He was taking in $500,000 from 1,000 customers with 2,000 prospective customers in his sales funnel. What if he was able to close 10% more bids and generate 1,100 customers out of his 2,000 prospects? His revenues would jump to $550,000 and his profits would rise from $30,000 to $46,000 (a 50% increase).

One reason for this large jump in profits is that he would be spending less money on marketing cost to do it. He would became more efficient at doing what he was already doing. If he were to just market more he would also earn more customers but his profits would be less due to his variable cost from placing more ads.

Joe created a comprehensive training program. Part of that program included having review sessions with craftsmen after each of their first ten jobs and randomly afterward. He started posting a ranking system in the office for the craftsmen based on criteria including customer service, lack of complaints, customer testimonials and upselling with awards of gas cards given to his top craftsmen.

	Start	Add 10% Conversion
Prospects	2,000	2,000
Conversion Rate	50%	55%
# of Customers	1,000	1,100
Price	$500	$500
Repeat Customers	1.0	1.0
Total Revenues	$500,000	$ 550,000
Profit Margin	6.0%	8.4%
Profits	$30,000	$46,000

Figure 25. Increase Conversions 10%

Joe changed how he managed his office and his contractors. He started spending more time in the field. He started going on customer visits with his craftsmen, especially the newer contractors. He started making unannounced visits to customers' homes while his craftsmen were working and he started making final walk-through visits with the craftsmen and his customers when the jobs were complete.

Over a few months major changes occurred. Joe found that he was closing more sales. He was also closing larger jobs and he was getting more referrals and repeat business. He had focused on the problem of closing sales. Also, by getting out of his comfort zone and challenging his staff he was able to upgrade their skills and their morale.

Joe found that by starting with quality personnel and demanding only the best he was able to start attracting higher and higher quality craftsmen. He was able to bring on board those who wanted to showcase their customer service skills and who wanted to work with someone who appreciated them as well.

Joe also worked with his office staff. He already had them using scripts when talking to customers but he worked with them to upgrade the phone scripts, to make them more realistic and so they would not sound like they were just read. He worked with them on the meaning of customer service, closing sales, asking customers for the order and talking about benefits rather than features.

By running the practice scenarios in the office with the craftsmen during the training sessions they also began teaming up with the craftsmen who in turn were better able to appreciate what the staff did for them in support. Improving his conversion ratio was a big step in turning his business into a Profit Machine.

Chapter 6

Price

The total amount of money a customer spends on your product per sale is the Price. It does not necessarily refer to the cost of one product but to the basket of goods bought at one time. At a grocery store it means the value of your shopping cart. At Amazon.com it means the book or books you just downloaded. At Handyman Joe's business it means a written contract for a repair or renovation job.

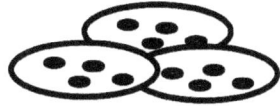

Figure 26. Price

Pricing items is an art and can cause inordinate headaches for the business owner. You need to know what your competition is charging and decide what your price point is relative to that. Or if your product is unique you have to figure out what the demand is by trial and error or using pricing tests in different areas in the market.

The price you can charge has a lot to do with the type of business you are operating. If you have a high quality, high service business with a luxury product you can charge a high price. If you have a low-cost, commodity-type product and you are competing on price then you must meet or beat your price competition. You can be a Rolex or a Mercedes-Benz or you can be a Wal-Mart.

Each has its pluses and minuses. To compete on price you will have low profit margins and you have to make up in volume what you lose in margin. Note that Wal-Mart, Target, Marshall's and the like are always running sales and spending a lot of money to entice customers to come in as often as possible. They work hard with their vendors to reduce their costs and their margins are, not much better than grocery stores; around 3.5%. This means that they have to bring in $100 in revenues to earn $3.50 in profits. On the other hand the profit margin for Mercedes-Benz is 8%. A small business needs profits of 20 -50% to sustain itself.

If you have a luxury brand and you avoid selling on price you can more easily ignore the competition's pricing and talk to your customers about the benefits of using your product instead of just the price. But you have to maintain high product and service standards and be willing to stand behind your product with a strong guarantee. Of course the Walmarts and the Targets of the world have guarantees too but they may not be administered well due to cost constraints.

Competing on Price

Avoid competing on price. In fact consider the benefits of raising your prices. You also want to avoid going into head-to-head competition with your competitors on price. Getting into a price war only hurts your business unless you are strong enough to go for a period of time losing money until your competitor goes out of business instead of you.

It can be a scary proposition to stop yourself from negotiating your price down. However, the customers who are solely concerned with price also tend to be "difficult" customers and perhaps you are better off without them. These are the ones who, following Pareto's rule (Investopedia, n.d.), are the 20% who take up 80% of your time and energy dealing with issues that are not necessarily real issues.

> Handyman Joe found that customers for his handyman business would often talk about price first but still expect top quality, a guarantee and high service levels. The sales

conversation would usually begin with the customer asking for Joe's hourly rates. The hourly rate is the way most customers have to compare bids in the absence of direct experience with a craftsman's skill and honesty. Joe worked by contract not by the hour, though. He used an hourly rate internally for his craftsmen to price out the contract not as a bargaining chip.

The reliance on hourly rate is a problem for the customer because the hourly craftsman would often inflate his hours after lowballing the bid to get the job. Using a fixed price contract, the final price would not change unless the scope of the job changed. The downside is that when they underbid a job sometimes poor craftsmanship would result on the part of his crew who felt underpaid.

Joe's craftsmen would also often fall into the trap of bargaining on price instead of highlighting their workmanship and the other benefits of working with his company. When they would present the bid often the conversation would be about how the homeowner could get the guy down the street to do the job for $25 per hour or even a case of beer.

The craftsmen would be unprepared to handle this objection. When Joe started working with them to improve their sales skills he taught them to talk about the benefits of working with a company that had been around for many years, had a guarantee, an A+ rating with the Better Business Bureau and had the resources to correct any problems if they occurred. Once they focused on those facts the price issue declined in importance as the benefits started outweighing the price in the mind of the customer.

There were customers whose only consideration was price. Although they demanded top-quality work, they weren't willing to pay for it. This would lead to differences of opinion between these customers and the people doing the work. Those customers who kept demanding lower prices and even kept bargaining on price after the contract was signed were customers that Joe and his crew started avoiding.

Make sure you appeal to those people who will appreciate your service. Be prepared to fire a customer who is not fair to you when you are trying to be fair to them (keeping in mind that you are not in the business of upsetting customers as a rule). On the other hand be prepared to "eat" a job that has gone sour and hold fast to your ethical principles. Your ability to delight an otherwise disgruntled customer can turn her into an advocate instead of a detractor.

Bundling and Upselling

Price is more than just the price tag. If you look at it as the total of the customer's shopping cart it can include much more than the cost of just one item. How many products do you sell? Are they related in some way? Can you develop more products or ancillary services to go along with your current line?

When you go into a McDonald's you see a menu with an array of à la carte products listed along with bundled meals. The meals are less expensive than the individual products bought separately. Why sell products at a discount like that? It seems counterproductive and goes against my admonition to never discount.

One factor is choice. People tend to be overwhelmed when faced with too many choices. Given two or three options rather than dozens makes it easier to pick. Bundled meals do this for consumers.

The larger reason is that it is lucrative for the business. A bundled meal, while appearing to save the buyer money actually tends to encourage him to consume more. While this is not beneficial for consumers' waistlines it is a way to generate more revenues and more profits for McDonalds.

Upsizing generates higher profits as well. When the customer buys a larger size fries or soda than he originally intended the business has just increased its price to the customer. The extra increment earns more profit for the business as long as the items are high profit margin products. Again the customer feels he is getting a deal since the cost to him is less than if he had purchased the same amount at regular price.

When you "Supersize" your fries, you are paying a small increment of extra money that makes purchasing the regular size appear to be more expensive. To spend a few cents more makes the purchase more economical in terms of cost per ounce of fries.

Figure 27. The Profitability of Upsizing

The cost to the company to produce a high margin product like French fries is negligible in terms of raw materials (a couple of cents' worth of potato and a bit more for a slightly larger container). The fixed cost is paid for by the price of the smaller product so in essence the extra fifty cents for extra-large fries is nearly pure profit.

Restaurants practice Upselling to improve profits. The staff is trained to make suggestions to customers to add items to their meal such as side orders, alcoholic beverages and desserts. They also suggest more expensive items or items that need to be sold before they go bad.

A restaurant may set the table for a full three-course meal to suggest to the customer an appetizer and a dessert are an expected part of the meal. The upselling process is vital for restaurants and hotels as a recent survey found. (Gerrard, 2012)

What can you do to add value for your customers so you can increase your total price and improve your profitability? If the food industry overwhelmingly finds this necessary how can you turn this concept to your advantage as well?

If you have written a book could there be a workbook added that can go along with it? How about a book on tape that can be played when having a paper book would be inconvenient? For a small extra fee that can be included in the price of the physical book and since the extra cost to produce it is negligible you earn profit on every sale.

> When Handyman Joe went along on customer site visits with his craftsmen he noticed that they would usually concentrate totally on the job the customer called about without looking around to see what else might need repair.

The interesting thing was that quite often, right when the initial customer visit was finishing up and the craftsman getting ready to leave, the customer would ask, "What about this rotted window sill? Or, do you paint (or do plumbing, or do tiling)?. Again, his craftsmen would often fail to follow up on these questions letting potential work get away.

Joe tried to get his workers to see that it made their lives easier and earned them more money if they would just look around the house as they headed to the area the customer wanted to be repaired and if they would take action on customers' questions about more work..

Joe trained his crew to ask, "What else is there I can help you with?" They were trained to keep asking "What else?" until the customer ran out of answers. The results were called into the office with the information about the customer's response to the bid and logged in for follow-up if they could not be dealt with right away. This was how Joe upsold and bundled products for his business.

Raising Prices

What would happen if you raised the price of your product? You may have the feeling that all of your customers would just run away never to return. In fact you may be surprised to find that most of your customers will remain loyal to you. Some will leave especially if price overrides quality and service as purchasing factors in their minds.

If you are in a highly competitive business with many others selling similar products of similar quality you may be constrained from raising your prices. If you are in a niche business with few competitors then you have more leeway.

Simply raising prices may or may not work for you but you should analyze your current pricing. Fundamentally, is the price you charge greater than all of your costs? I hope so or else you will be out of business soon. This is where using monthly business P&L reports are helpful. At the bottom of the report is it red ink or is it black?

If you are making a profit is it enough profit for you?

If not why are you in this business?

If you have more than one product does each one stand on its own?

> When I bought my restaurant I calculated the cost of every one of my dozens of products. I found that the previous owners had no real understanding of their profitability. Some products were profitable but some, although very popular, were money losers. Raising prices high enough to make them profitable priced them out of the market and they were taken off the menu.

Sometimes having a loss leader is OK as a sales promotion to bring in customers but if you make it a habit you may end up stuck in a continual sale unable to raise the price back up where it belongs.

Often when we price products we are just looking at the cost of the raw materials – the Cost of Goods Sold. Quite often we forget to factor in the overhead costs. Remember it is only after you reach breakeven that you earn a profit.

Later in this book we talk about Breakeven Point. Calculate your breakeven point for all of your products then look at your pricing. Are you earning enough money in profits to support your price points? If not can you raise your prices to earn enough profit? If not are you in the right business?

Here is an example of raising prices from Handyman Joe:

> When Joe raises his prices to his customers what happens?
> A 10% price increase results in 10% more revenues which
> you would expect. But a 10% price increase does not also
> result in a 10% increase in profits. In this case his profits
> increased by over 50% from $30,000 to $46,000 and his
> profit margin increases from 6% to 8%.
>
> Why is that? It is because Joe has already sold enough of
> his services that his fixed costs are already paid off. After
> that point 68% of his revenues pay his variable costs – his
> contract workers, his royalties, his warranty issues, etc.

	Start	Add 10% Price
Prospects	2,000	2,000
Conversion Rate	50%	50%
# of Customers	1,000	1,000
Price	$500	$550
Repeat Customers	1.0	1.0
Total Revenues	$500,000	$550,000
Profit Margin	6.0%	8.4%
Profits	$30,000	$46,000

Figure 28. Profits from Price Increase

The remaining 32% is now profit. If you think about
paying off your overhead expenses or fixed costs first
every month you will understand why you must be careful
of increasing your expenses or decreasing your prices.
Every extra penny of overhead expense or revenue

reduction from discounting comes right out of your profits.

If you raise your prices you earn more profits. However, you have to balance your price against what your customers are willing to pay. If you offer a superior product in terms of performance and in your customer service you can charge a higher price.

If you have competitors in your niche you cannot charge as high a price as you would like. Your product must also have enough value to your customers to be worth the cost in the mind of the customer. Instead of just raising prices there are other, better ways to generate more income from your customers.

Discounting

One time-honored way to get customers into the door is to reduce your prices – have a sale or hand out discount coupons. It can be tempting to offer a sale, to get people in the door. You do have to pay your overhead costs no matter what. There may be times when you need to generate cash flow so you can pay off your inventory costs. However, discounting has so many negative sides to it that I normally recommend against it.

When you tell people you are willing to reduce your price you are telling them that your product was overpriced in the first place. Customers may even feel insulted that you wouldn't give them your best price right off the bat.

If you discount your price you are also telling the customer that your product is cheap. Not low-priced but cheaply made or shoddy. Be careful of the message you are sending to your customer. What about the customer who bought your product at the regular price and now you are selling it for less? Now the Law of Unintended Consequences catches up to you and you may have angered a customer instead of pleasing him.

Law of Unintended Consequences

This is what happens when you plan to do something and something else jumps out catching you unawares and bites you on your rear.

> An example of The Law of Unintended Consequences is the woman in England who intended to market her business with a Groupon (Brown, 2011) for 75% off for a dozen cupcakes. The offer was so desirable it went crazy viral and she was forced to make over 100,000 cupcakes at a loss of $20,000, nearly bankrupting her. Unfortunately, as a marketing tool it did not work as few of those customers ever returned for the full-price versions. (Bhasin, 2011).

When you start reducing your price you start drawing attention to it – just the opposite of what you really want. You want to take the focus off of the price and onto the benefits of your product. You make a superior product right? Well, if it's so good then why are you having a fire sale to get it off your shelves?

This is where a thorough understanding of your product's features and benefits is necessary. What problems does your product solve? What pain does it remove for your customer? Every time the shopper focuses on price you must move the focus to the benefits.

> Earlier in the book we learned how Handyman Joe worked with his craftsmen to stop talking about price and focus on the benefits of their work. They wrote up their quotes and went over them with their customers making sure that they and their customers understood the scope of the work.

They talked to the customers about the written guarantee on the back of every contract, where they would take the leftover trash and the cost to do so and whether they were picking up materials for the customer. They talked about the fact that they were vetted before they started work. They showed the customer their "Brag" book with photos of previous jobs and talked about their past successes.

Then they presented the price, asked for the order and stopped talking. Not talking is a valuable tool. Nobody likes "dead air." This puts the onus on the customer to make some kind of decision then and there. If they got a "no" they would move on to the next job leaving it up to the office to make further contacts with the customer asking about the job. A "yes" and they would get a signature on the contract and then start work immediately.

Joe was able to raise his prices not by charging more per hour but by earning more work from his customers for each job performed. Instead of one call for minimum price work the now well-trained craftsmen were able to get higher paying jobs and repeat business from loyal customers. Customers were able to trust Joe's crew more easily when they presented themselves on a more professional level and stopped comparing themselves to their competition.

Joe used $100 per hour as his internal rate to calculate his overall price for the job. There were many other competitors who were using that or more as their hourly rate but there were also plenty of other craftsmen competing with him at $20-$25 per hour. Interestingly, the competitors' final prices to their customers were often quite close to Joe's bids once all the hours and "unforeseen" extras were taken into account.

In this business craftsmen are notorious for being untrustworthy and often disappear or get fired before completing their job. Somebody else then has to finish or even completely redo the work. Of course this ends up costing the customer more than what Joe would have charged from the beginning and with a lot less hassle.

By concentrating on the benefits, reassuring his customers that they were covered in the event of failure, by putting testimonials on his website, by showing his craftsmen how to be better salesmen he was able to sell his services without having to lower his prices.

When is it OK to discount? You may have excess inventory and it is costing you more in storage fees to hold it or it may be last year's product and the latest version needs to start selling. You may need cash flow to pay for raw materials or other costs.

You may be starting out and establishing your name. Be careful of discounting your name in addition to your product as we have discussed above. If you make discounting a habit now you may find yourself unable to raise your prices later.

The Folly of Discounting – An Example

What happens when you change your prices? What happens when you discount your product to make a sale? What happens when you raise prices?

Let's look at an example from Handyman Joe.

Handyman Joe's craftsman negotiates with a customer to perform a job that will take him an estimated 15 hours to complete. His initial price is calculated based on $100/hr = $1,500 to the customer. The customer negotiates a 10% price reduction to $1,350 and the craftsman accepts.

If he had won the job at $1,500 Handyman Joe would have earned $90 net profit.

With the $150 revenue opportunity lost he needs to recalculate his profits based on the original bid of $1,500. Why?

- Reducing revenues to $1,350 means that the office still has to support the craftsman for a 15 hour job

- The craftsman has to work 15 hours to get paid for 13.5 hours' worth of work so he loses money.

- By working 15 hours to complete the job the craftsman and the office staff are not available that extra 1.5 hours to work on other jobs

Instead of a net profit of $90 he actually earned only $42 – just half of his original profit.

In the example below you can see what happens when this job is discounted by one third. You might think that you can still squeak by with a small profit or at least not lose money but here a $90 profit has now turned into a $70 loss – a swing from a 6% profit to a 7% loss.

If discounting is a way of life for your business find out the real cost and think about your lost opportunities. You think you are earning so much in profits but then you look in your bank account at the end of the month scratching your head, wondering where all the money went.

The moral of the story with discounting is to know your numbers beforehand and know how low you can go before you are willing to call off a negotiation.

Discounting & Net Profit

Discount	0%	-10%	-33%
Total Revenues	$1,500	$1,350	$1,000
Variable Costs @ 68%	-$1,020	-$ 918	-$ 680
Gross Profit	$ 480	$ 432	$ 320
Fixed Costs	-$ 390	-$ 390	-$ 390
$ Net Profit	$ 90	$ 42	-$ 70
% Net Profit	6%	3%	-7%

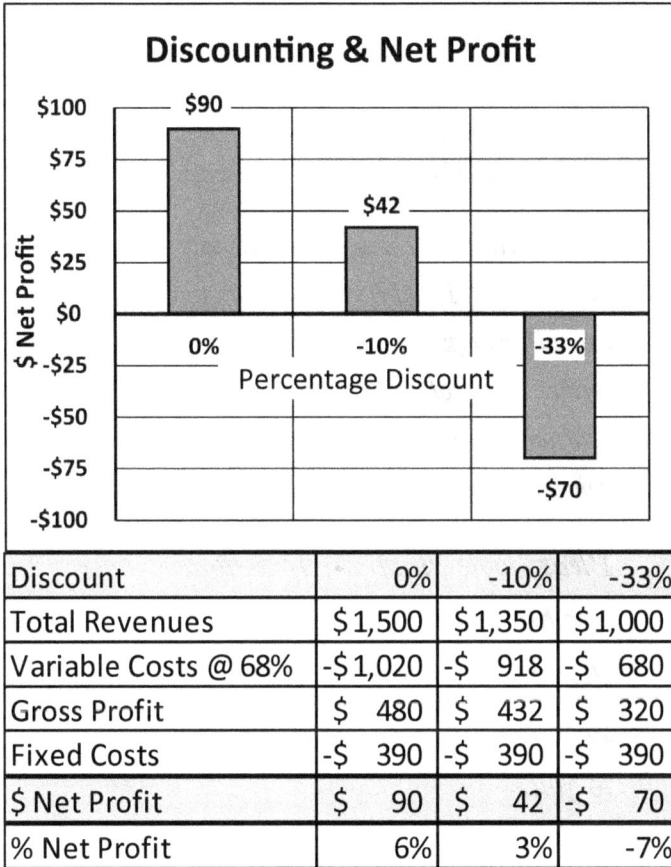

Figure 29. Discounting Example

There may be times when cash flow is important and you may be willing to settle for just covering your variable costs. If that is the case realize that you are losing money with the transaction and in the long run it is untenable.

Your goal is to find ways to increase your price to your customer. You can increase your prices or bundle products. Avoid discounting to win customers. Counter a Price argument by concentrating on the benefits to the customer:

> "Well Ma'am, I'd love to give you a lower price on this product but I hope you can appreciate that in order to provide you with our high level of product quality and service I cannot charge any less. I know that you will find that our product is worth every penny you spend on it once you have tried it."

> Please look at what our customers have said about our product on our testimonials page. Don't forget that we offer a written 100% satisfaction guarantee so you can purchase our product at entirely no risk to you."

Chapter 7

Repeat Sales – Customer Service

How many times in your life have you felt delighted by a buying experience? Not just satisfied or even happy but just plain delighted. Sadly, it does not happen very often but when it does you are left with a memorable experience.

What would it be worth to you to feel that you were the center of the universe of the company you are dealing with? Would you want to return there? Would you tell others about your treatment and encourage them to shop there as well? Would you be willing to pay even more for the experience?

Now think about all those times when you were met with indifference, poor service, even downright rudeness and hostility. Why would you want to return to a place of business that presents you with that kind of service?

Sometimes businesses seem to actually throw up barriers to doing business with them all the while they are proclaiming their great customer service. They just

Figure 30. Returning Customers

don't seem to get it. If you return it is because you have to, not because you want to. To turn your business into a Profit Machine you must begin and end with impeccable service.

Quibbling over a few dollars or arguing about whether a customer is right or wrong is a sure way to create a poor aura around your business. Word of mouth works much swifter and harsher for negative experiences than the opposite for good ones

An upset customer will tell 24 others about their bad experience and a happy one will tell 9. (Katie Smith Milway, 2005) With the speed and breadth of social media it can quickly become a nightmare once a negative campaign about your business starts.

In a survey of over 350 businesses and their customers (Katie Smith Milway, 2005) 80% of the companies said they deliver superior service yet only 8% of their customers agreed. Customer service is one of the first things to go when corporations work to reduce costs as it is something that appears to be a drain on profit without a tangible benefit.

Of course your business is in the 8% right? How do you know that? We will talk about measurement of customer satisfaction later in this chapter but first let's talk about how to earn your customers' loyalty and get them to come back and buy more and more.

Are you Deluding Yourself About Your Customer Service Performance?

Think about the best customer service experiences you have had. Did it feel like they were genuine, not forced or phony? Did it feel like they had your best interest at heart? Or did they quibble over a dollar? Did they make you feel like you were family welcoming you with open arms? Did they make you feel like a bad experience was not a burden but a problem to be solved and resolved as quickly as possible in your favor?

If you are unsure of the value of repeat business look at your cost in money and time to generate one new customer. Write it down.

What is your sales and marketing cost targeting new business? How much time do spend networking and following up to get people through the door.

If it costs you less time and effort to bring in new customers than to get existing customers to come back then go ahead and keep targeting new business. How many new people can you reach though? Could you run out of new customers to target?

Your first sale to a new customer may end up as a loss leader. You may set up your business deliberately to create repeat business. Repeat business is where you can earn much greater profit. Acquire new customers for expanding your business and to replace customers who have stopped buying.

Often we let our customers walk away and keep putting all of our efforts into purchasing new customers with our marketing dollars rather than trying to keep the ones we have. Why is that? Do we assume that those people who have purchased from us don't need any more of our product? Do we assume that they know all about us and will just automatically walk back in when they want more? Are we simply afraid to ask them for more business?

We may be worried that if we ask our customers for more business we are just going to annoy them. But in reality, if you are happy with a product wouldn't you feel somewhat flattered if you were reminded of your good judgement in buying that product?

How would you create an atmosphere that not just invites but entices customers back for more? To do this first you need to have superlative customer service and you need a product that invites more sales.

Gillette created a whole new idea in marketing when they introduced the "loss-leader" concept of selling the handle of the razor so they had a continuous, lifetime customer buying custom designed disposable blades to fill it. The product was superior in that the disposable blade did not have to be sharpened and the initial purchase price was much lower than for a straight razor.

Today you see this concept in computer printers that are inexpensive to buy but have to have expensive proprietary ink cartridge refills. For Gillette razors the lifetime cost of the blades is much more than the handle they fit in and much more than the cost of an old-fashioned permanent straight razor.

The example of a book as a one-time sale is an example. If your book is good enough you may entice people to buy copies for friends. Writing sequels, selling workbooks or just writing more books encourage your satisfied customers to keep on coming back for more.

E-books are often issued now in serial format with a free introductory volume as an inducement to get into the theme (the loss-leader concept again). Then, once readers are involved and interested in the story, they have to keep purchasing the sequels as the story progresses. So instead of one large tome at one large price there are many small books, almost chapters or at least novellas in size for a lower individual cost.

The key is that the author has to provide a story that is worthy of waiting for the next chapter and worth the incremental cost. Anticipation makes you want the next chapter even more. When you add up the cost of all the installments you realize you have spent far more than you would have for a single volume book issued at a much later date when it was complete.

Because many e-books are self-published the product quality can slip with typos and plot holes left unedited. This creates dissatisfaction and potentially loss of customers. The e-book industry works off of book reviews with positive reviews generating more sales so the ability to entice customers to post reviews is part of the publishing process now.

New Customer Acquisition Cost

How much does it cost you to earn the business of a new customer? If you don't know already you should start keeping track of how much it costs you to bring in new customers.

Although Social Media can be "free" of charge to use for your Marketing efforts it comes at a cost of your valuable time to post and repost, to engage and to become part of the Community you are targeting so you should put a cost of your time on those effort.

Use the accompanying New Customer Acquisition Cost Form to determine the cost to earn a new customer and compare it to the cost to keep an old one.

A. Marketing Cost for New Customers $_____

B. Number of New Customers _____

Acquisition Cost = A. $_____ / B. _____ = $_____

Write down how much it costs to bring in a repeat customer.

C. Marketing For Repeat Customers $_____

D. Number of Repeat Visits by Existing Customers _____

Repeat Customer Cost = C. $_____ / D. _____= $_____

Which is larger? Which makes more sense to pursue for your
   business?

Figure 31. New Customer Acquisition Cost Form

What happened with Handyman Joe's customers?

It costs Handyman Joe $50 to acquire each new customer on average and $10 to encourage repeat customers. He earns an average of $500 per customer in revenues with a 6% profit margin netting $30 for a new customer.

It turned out that when he bought the business there were few customers calling him back after the first job was done. Most of the work was just one-time contracts.

Joe wasn't looking for one sale though, he was looking for a second, third and fourth sale from each customer. He wanted the lifetime business of that customer. If all of Joe's customers were to suddenly become repeat customers he would earn $70 in profits per customer for a 12% profit margin.

This means that with 1,000 customers he would then earn 50% more business. Joe's problem was that he was not getting the amount of repeat business he needed so his profit margin suffered and his business was floundering. The causes of his lack of repeat business could be traced to his customer service.

	Start	Add 10% Repeat Customer
Prospects	2,000	2,000
Conversion Rate	50%	50%
# of Customers	1,000	1,000
Price	$500	$500
Repeat Customers	1.0	1.1
Total Revenues	$500,000	$550,000
Profit Margin	6.0%	8.4%
Profits	$30,000	$46,000

Figure 32. Increase Repeat Customers by 10%

Supreme Customer Service

Besides Profit the ultimate reward for you as a business owner should be that your customers want to come back to your store and buy your product again and again. This is a testament to your superb product and service quality.

There are companies whose business model is to deliberately serve a customer once and do not care if they return. These are businesses that keep costs so low that they are understaffed and underequipped. They provide little or no training for their employees, feeling that it is an unnecessary cost. These are businesses built for the short-term. They are businesses that the owners do not care if they fail or not.

> Handyman Joe had to compete with craftsmen who were legitimate and with those who were not. The bad actors caused problems for the construction business in general.
>
> Prospective customers associated him with the problem contractors and did not understand how hard he worked to earn his A+ Better Business Bureau rating and they would transfer their anger about past jobs gone badly to him.
>
> He found the mistrust of contractors was quite rampant but also found people who were victimized over and over by those who sought to simply take rather than provide a decent service.
>
> Joe was proud of his efforts to treat his customers well. He had many testimonials from happy customers affirming how he had helped them and how he had rescued customers who had been maltreated by other craftsmen.

By providing the utmost in customer service you can set yourself apart from the rest of your competitors. Cherish your customers. Make them feel like you would like to feel. The way to do this is through your employees.

What do your or your staff say when they talk to your prospective and current customers? Remember your current customers will influence future sales by either buying or not buying your products again or through telling their friends and family about your product and support. Do you know exactly how those interactions will go? If not then you need to look at your sales training and how you script your contacts.

People often think that using scripts sounds like they are reading from a piece of paper and that it comes across poorly. Sometimes that is true. An unmotivated, uncaring employee who is just reading some lines is not a good ambassador for your operation.

But done the right way scripts can free you up from having to think through everything they say and instead concentrate on using your brainpower to figure out how to solve customer problems and take advantage of opportunities as they arise.

> I have used scripts in my businesses and found them to be liberating. It is necessary to interject animation when speaking but when I do not use scripts when answering the phone I make mistakes, there are a lot of 'ers and 'ums and the flow is not good.

> When I use a script I make sure that everybody hears exactly the same thing and I know that if a customer has an issue that they have heard about my product, my guarantee, how to purchase and how to pay.

How do you respect your potential customers? First by the appearance of yourself and your office. Next by general demeanor and speech. Do you greet every customer as they walk in? How many times have you walked into an office or a store and been completely ignored until the admin or clerk got off the phone or finished chatting with someone else without even a glance of acknowledgement that you were there?

Your first priority is to greet the new arrival and make her feel welcomed. A quick interruption of your current call or talk may be necessary. Just stop for a second to let them know you will be right with them. Even looking up with a quick nod to acknowledge her presence.

The same goes for a website or a phone call. If someone makes an enquiry by email or text you need to get right back to them. I have had customers bowled over when I returned an email or a message within a few minutes and to be honest it shouldn't be that odd of an occurrence.

If you can, answer a phone call by the 2nd ring. If you need it to go to voicemail don't have the phone ring five times then go to a voicemail system that rings another five times. And don't use automated answering systems without a usable option to talk to a real, live human being. You may save on expenses with an automated phone system but you will probably never know how many sales you have lost from people who gave up trying to reach you.

Don't send customers into "voicemail hell" as I call it, where you are given cryptic choices then have no way to even leave a message. Or you hit the number for reception and nobody answers or you get a directory that requires that you know the extension number, etc. etc. etc. No matter how big you get you should try to deal with customers directly.

> I was returning home on the last ferry of the day recently and a fellow passenger came up and asked if she could borrow my cell phone to make a call. She needed to

contact her motel as it would be after hours when she and her husband got there and she was afraid they would be closed by that time.

I handed her the phone and she got the aforementioned voicemail hell. It was only about 10:45 and the voice told her that after 11:00 there would be no front desk service and to punch in the number for the manager's extension. She did just that and the manager's extension forwarded her back to the front desk automated number. I tried it as well and clearly there was no way to speak to a live person to ensure that they could check in late and no way to even leave a message. I told her that there was a motel across the street in case they were left out in the cold.

If that was you would you accept that behavior? Would you return to that place of business or recommend it to your friends? What kind of rating would you post about it? Perhaps there was an emergency at the motel. More likely the manager decided not to deal with customers and wanted to go to bed even though he knew he had a customer coming who had not checked in yet.

The accompanying Customer Service Process Map on page 137 is available as a checklist to ensure that you have a robust customer service process for your business. Use this to make sure that you have the structure that puts your customers first.

Do you really want to deal with an irate customer with an off-the-cuff response? Do you want your customers to meet staff members who don't follow a dress code or who stand around chatting rather than serving? Do you or your office staff know the importance of telephone etiquette and the role of the office admin staff in sales?

Be one of the 8% of businesses who earn their customers' respect and generate massive repeat business through word of mouth.

Training

Employee training is where high-quality customer service begins and ends. Anybody who in any way touches the customer is a representative of your business. Whether you are a solopreneur or head of a large corporation it is incumbent on every employee or contractor to present the best face toward the customer and toward any stakeholders in your business.

In a retail operation the store staff is there to provide sales support, help customers find what they are looking for, reduce the probability of theft and to encourage the customer to buy the store's products.

Yet what do we encounter in high-end boutiques as well as the big box department store? Indifference. Staff members chatting with each other or on the phone or just not there at all. No greeting, no offer to help. Or if there is it is perfunctory with an air that the customer is an annoyance to be gotten rid of as soon as possible.

Do you, as the business owner, think you are immune? Do you think that when you are away that your staff is perky and happy and focusing on the customer to the exclusion of all else?

This is why mystery shoppers have become popular with business owners. Store visits are made by people who look like typical customers who are there to rate the business on customer service. They are there to ferret out the good and bad about a store's service levels. Owners are often surprised at what they find.

To achieve superior customer service you need staff who are motivated to achieve and who care. It is easy to take a good worker and turn them into a poor one. It is harder to go the other way. A good manager is one who cares about her staff and is always working with them to improve their skills not to berate them or bully them into compliance.

Starbucks is known for the way they train and motivate their staff. They take the time to make sure that a new employee has all the tools they need to not just make a latté but to engage customers, to head off complaints before the happen and to engage customers properly when they do.

Realize that Starbucks does not just sell overpriced coffee drinks. They sell an experience. A welcoming atmosphere, somewhat trendy and a bit snooty with French-named cup sizes and baristas making your drinks, a place to have a leisurely drink and a chat with a friend or to grab a personally made beverage of your choice, made the way you want it.

You go to buy a cup of coffee. You receive a pleasant experience with a group of like-minded people in a clean and welcoming environment and leave feeling happy.

In order to generate that experience for their customers they concentrate on their staff. First of all they have an extended medical package for their employees, even part-timers who normally are not eligible so they can hire higher quality workers than their competitors. Each new employee undergoes at least 24 - 40 hours of training in how to recognize and respond to customer needs. They learn about the company's process for dealing with unpleasant situations (and really, would you have them call it anything else?).

Starbucks baristas and managers learn to use the LATTE method to recognize when their customers are exhibiting negative emotions and, more importantly, how to address these emotions in positive ways. (Duhigg, 2012),

We:

 Listen to the customer,

Acknowledge the complaint,

Take action by solving the problem,

Thank them and then

Explain why the problem occurred

Figure 33. The LATTE Method

What can we learn from this process? Customer service training goes beyond the mechanics of using a cash register and pressing a button on an automated expresso maker. Customer service training in the Starbucks world is about empowering employees. They are trained how to deal with customer complaints through empathy and how to best respond to customer concerns. Employees feel confident that they are backed by management and not second-guessed.

As entrepreneurs part of our stereotypical makeup is to be micro-managers. We want things to go right and we are driven to succeed convinced that the right way is our way. It's personal because it's our money and our success of failure on the line.

In our quest for success we often tread over people without even knowing we do. When hiring employees it is possible to treat them like chess pieces moving them about without thought to their feelings. It is also possible to go the other way and just let them do whatever they want without recourse.

As a leader you have to lead. You have to make decisions and occasionally cut loose people who will not follow your lead. You cannot play favorites. Favoritism is a sure way to destroy the morale of an organization.

Ideally you want to create a structure for your office or store that is easy to follow and allows for staff members to have some level of control over their work. When you are developing your customer service process you really need to involve your staff. The more you understand the issues your staff face and the more you listen to them the more workable your system will be.

> In union contract negotiations the chemical production company I worked with was negotiating with the union to change from 8 hour to 12 hour shifts. We had a simple four days on days, four days off and four nights on arrangement planned. My unionized Operations crew came up with a very offbeat and complex shift schedule that gave them seven days off in a row. It would have been easy to just dismiss their plan as unworkable but I could see a huge morale boost to encouraging their involvement and initiative.

> My one challenge to them was that they ensure that there was no shift to be left without an operator in case someone called in sick since on 12 hour shifts a gap could not be covered by holding one shift over and bringing in the other early as you can on 8 hour shifts. They took on that challenge and they were so enthusiastic that I never had a problem with shift coverage. It helped to ensure that a complex and potentially dangerous operation was run by relatively happy and motivated workers.

If you listen to people they will do a lot for you in return. It is your job to make decisions that will make your business work and you do not want to abdicate that role. By listening to your employees they will feel much more part of your team and will enthusiastically support you. The more decision-making you can put into their hands for those things that are inconsequential to the operation of your business the better.

I have been in organizations where managers felt they had to make every decision no matter how small. These are the micromanagers and if you work for one of them your life can be hell. Nothing you do is good enough. There is always criticism and rarely encouragement. I have also worked in situations where the manager believed so wholeheartedly in consensus they never made a decision unless everybody bought into it leading to no decisions at all.

The first person creates a disgruntled workforce of disenchanted drones. The second creates a workforce of entitled prima donnas who follow no rules unless they feel happy with them.

If you abdicate your authority you will have no control over the situation and you will not be able to ensure that your customers are all delighted by their experience. It may not be easy but there are times when it is necessary to say no or to correct or retrain behaviors. On the other hand the more decision-making authority you can entrust your staff with the easier it is to get employee buy-in into your vision and to feel loyalty toward you.

Whenever you are called upon to make a decision ask yourself if you really need to. If you have policies and procedures in place you can reference them instead of trying to make up responses to situations off the top of your head. On the one hand you want a script for how to manage customer relations. On the other, giving employees authority to deal with situations such as unhappy customers is empowering.

Customer Relations Management

How do you want to handle customers? Are you OK with staff standing around chatting and talking on the phone or texting? How would you deal with a situation like that? You customer service training process will set the stage for how customers are managed. It helps to have a script and have you and your staff use it. It's OK to have variations but stick within that scope.

> When Handyman Joe took over his handyman business it came with a staff person who refused to use the company scripts she was given. She chatted on the phone when the craftsmen called in their bids thereby missing calls from customers. She chatted with customers as well, discussing her personal business with them.
>
> Because she spent so much time chatting she did not get other work done in the office. Joe received complaints from customers about how they were treated. Even his craftsmen were not happy because she took up time they needed to use to do paying work.
>
> After trying unsuccessfully to get her to address the issues Joe put her on a performance improvement plan. He set up goals and even had her time her phone usage over a period of time. Unfortunately, she did not change her habits and he had to let her go.
>
> His subsequent hires were trained to use the scripts, followed procedures (even helping to develop them) and the efficiency of the office went up. Joe started getting compliments about his office rather than complaints.

Every part of the customer process should be walked through and responses scripted. (Use the Customer Service Process Map on page 135). How do you deal with customer complaints? Is it all ad hoc? Is there a specific process you go through to make sure the complaint is legitimate, that you understand fully what the complaint is and the scope of the problem? Is it an issue that your insurance company might need to be informed of? Are there legal ramifications?

How do you deal with an angry customer? How do you deal with a happy customer? Are you prepared to ask for repeat business? Are you prepared to ask for referrals? Do you have specials and coupons that callers should know about? How do you tell your staff about policy changes regarding customers? Do you document training?

How do you deal with a difficult employee? How do you deal with managing poor performance? How do you go about properly firing an employee so you don't end up having the courts tell you to rehire him?

How do you reward good performance? In the One Minute Manager (Ken Blanchard, 1982)) tells us:

> *"The Key to Developing People is to Catch*
> *Them Doing Something Right."*

We often go looking for what is wrong and are trying to correct it. How do you feel when someone berates you or always tells you that you are wrong? How do you feel when someone praises you? Would you prefer to run a business based on praise or based on scolding?

Set standards for attire. Have a written dress code. Have a written code of conduct. How strict do you need to be? Again, be fair. Don't let one person off the hook and berate the next for transgressions. But if you do not enforce your policies your staff will not take them seriously and you are better off not having them at all.

Go through scenarios with your staff. Do mock phone calls or sales. Pretend to be a difficult customer and role-play a number of times until everybody feels comfortable with the role. If you already have your policies in place for dealing with unhappy customers then you will have consistent responses that meet your requirements instead of off-the-cuff disasters.

Dealing with an unhappy customer takes patience. Train your employees that if they are dealing with an emotional situation let the person talk it out. If the customer becomes abusive the response is to tell them that you will not deal with them until they speak respectfully with you

 If you or your employee is in physical proximity to an angry customer you should already have a plan of escape and a plan to call the authorities. Review your physical office or store layout. Can people become trapped by an irate customer?

Train your employees on the benefits of your product. Why should customers buy? When would the product not be a good purchase? If a customer cannot find what they are looking for in your product where can they find an alternative?

What is your guarantee? What is your return policy? How much leeway does the employee have with dealing with customer service issues and when do they need to contact you?

Define your customer service model. Train your employees. Trust your employees. Give them positive as well as negative feedback. Keep records of performance. However, as much as you may like them or dislike them you are not their friend and you are not their adversary.

Recognize that nobody is irreplaceable. Keep in mind that you must be prepared to fire any given employee but keep it as a last resort not a threat held over employees' heads.

Why Do Customers Return?

Why should a customer return and buy your product again? What entices them to return to your place of business? Is your product a consumable that needs to be purchased again and again? Do you have one product and you will never sell another one to that person?

Once you set up a high-level customer service process what will your happy customers do? If you have done your job well they will become evangelists for you. They will preach your name to all and sundry. You will have created a lifetime customer who will trudge through snowdrifts in Manitoba to find you again.

You should encourage those customers who love your product or even if the just like your product. Ask them to come back again. Give them a reason to return.

Loyalty Programs

Set up a loyalty program. Although you don't want to be discounting your price you can certainly encourage customers to return by giving them an incentive to do so. Customer rewards programs are often used to create a sense of loyalty and desire to use a particular brand or store.

> I tend to use the same brand of gasoline, not because of price or quality, but because I have a rewards card and can use the points to reduce future purchase costs. The points I earn are worth about 1/10 of a penny per dollar I spend on the gas but I collect them nonetheless.

Coffee shops use the buy 10 and get the next cup free model and end up with customers so loyal they will get pretty upset if they can't locate their rewards card to get their stamp. Grocery stores give points to redeem or reduce the prices of select goods. (They also collect your buying habit data in the process).

The key to success with reward programs is that you have to celebrate the reward. If you get chintzy and try to avoid or downplay the reward it will backfire. Instead you need to ring a bell or make an announcement when the prize is awarded. Be generous and give out extra stamps on the coffee card if you can. It's like priming the pump in gambling. They have loud bells and whistles when someone hits the jackpot at the casinos.

Knowing that there is a solid payoff will keep customers returning again and again so they can get that reward as well. If you look stingy or if the prize is an illusion then customers will stay away in droves and you can lose more business than if you didn't have the program in the first place (see Law of Unintended Consequences above).

Create a special membership program just for your repeat customers. You can have coupons and specials just for them. You can give away coupons for affiliate stores that sell complementary (not competitive) products. You can add content to your website for download to keep customers coming back for more.

TOMA Revisited

Getting repeat business is a two-pronged issue. First of all you must impress your customer enough that they like your product and the way you handle their business that they like you. Then you need to make sure that they will think of you when they want to buy your product again.

> Handyman Joe had literally hundreds of competitors to his handyman business in his work area since anybody who can pick up a hammer can call themselves a craftsman. Some were just out for a quick buck. Some

were high quality professionals who were so good they only took on work through referrals. Most (but not all) of them worked a lot cheaper than Joe's guys would because Joe had office overhead costs to absorb.

So, how did Joe try to earn his customers' respect and repeat business? By producing consistently high quality work and by servicing the customers' needs. Often a craftsman off the street would be working in a neighborhood and the neighbors would see his truck and amble over and ask him about what he was doing then they would say, "Oh, by the way, could you look at this at my place?" That is how many craftsmen market their businesses.

In Joe's case, the office would handle a phone call from a prospect who had received his flyer and a trained staff member would talk to the customer. His scripts were designed to get information from the customer and to go over the fact that they used written contracts unlike most everybody else, that they had a guarantee they would honor if necessary and had other craftsmen who could handle the work just in case and that there was an office to handle any issues and follow up to make sure that the job was done right. It was the reassurance and the guarantee that people would appreciate and follow up on.

The customer experience with Handyman Joe's office showed he was professional and his craftsmen were trustworthy. When the craftsmen did the work and the customer was happy with how she was treated the cycle of repeat business was primed and ready to go.

Why would customers want to return to buy again and again from you? How do you make your own buying decisions? Often we will try a product because it is advertised and sounds good. Perhaps a friend has tried it. Or we search the internet and check the reviews online. Learn how to use that positive feeling about your product as social proof to make people feel comfortable about buying your product.

Using Customer Complaints to Generate Loyalty

Buying decisions may have nothing to do with the actual product. Customer experience with store personnel or the online store may be more important than the product itself.

> I was at a restaurant recently with my teenage son. We go there often and play cribbage while eating pizza. This time we decided not to get the pizza and instead he ordered Fettuccini Alfredo and I had a Lamb Gyro. His dish arrived hot and bubbling but mine was lukewarm and the meat looked like it was right out of a can of SPAM®, not what I would expect from this place especially considering the exorbitantly high prices they were charging.

> I had to flag down the waitress and instead of saying "sorry we'll take care of this" she told me that she had picked it right up from the kitchen so it should be OK. The manager came out then and said the kitchen was sure they did it right. Although they remade the dish it still wasn't right. At that point I gave up complaining.

> The waitress did not ask how the replacement meal was. When I went to pay I was not asked how my dinner was either. Now I don't know if I want to go back at all in spite of the good food I have had there in the past.

How could they have made that a positive experience? Perhaps this was a new waitress not being able to juggle all that is required with a new job. The manager, though, made it quite obvious that his focus was not on ensuring his customers enjoyed their experience. This is an organization in bad need of a shakeup and at the least a review of customer service policies.

On the other hand a different experience shows how good service engenders loyalty and ultimately repeat business and referral business:

> I was at another bar/restaurant with a large group of friends along with my partner. After her main course salad was served and she had eaten the top layer she found that the greens were wilted and unappetizing. She ate around it but was clearly not pleased.

> I flagged down the waiter as he was bussing the table. Even though she had already eaten a fair amount of the salad he immediately apologized, took the remainder of the salad back to the kitchen, offered to replace it and took it off the bill.

> His service during a very busy evening was also quite good, he was knowledgeable about the menu and made good recommendations to customers, was attentive, filing up water glasses and drinks and most importantly he made sure that we were pleased with our experience.

> There was no question of whether we were right or wrong – it was just that something was not to our liking – and he made it right. This is what earns customer loyalty. He didn't give us the dinner for free or bring drinks or dessert costing extra money for the business but took care of it and made us feel like they were happy we were there.

Often we think that we are serving our customers when in reality we are just delivering a product without thinking about what the customer is actually experiencing. What is the experience your customers have when they come into your store, log into your website or meet with you?

Are they welcomed with open arms? Do you know what they are likely to want or need from you? Will they be able to get in and out of your store easily and painlessly? How well-prepared are you at handling problems as they arise?

It is possible to create undying customer loyalty if you handle a complaint immediately and to the customer's satisfaction. It does not necessarily mean that you just give in but you need to look at what you win when you tell a customer "no."

Is it worth losing a customer over a $1, a $10 or even a $100 dispute? Perhaps. There are people who will try to take advantage of business owners and staff and you have to be prepared to manage those situations. Most customers just want a fair deal. Remember that you will rarely get complaints. Customers will simply walk away and you will never hear from them again – and they will tell 24 others about their unhappiness. A happy customer though will tell only 15. (AMEX, 2012)

Lagniappe

In the French Quarter in New Orleans in the Southern U.S. there is a term called, "Lagniappe." It means, "Something a little extra." Restaurants use this to provide a wonderful customer experience. It may take the form of an Amuse Bouche (a tiny appetizer) at the start of the meal or a free coffee or extra dessert. The 13th donut in a baker's dozen is that same idea.

As they say in New Orleans, "Laissez les bon temps rouler!" (Let the good times roll).

Providing customers with an unexpected extra is a sure way to generate goodwill. The idea is to make sure the customer has a wonderful experience, one that they will remember and keep them coming back again and again.

Setting Up a Customer-Service Oriented Business

What sets a customer-service-oriented business apart from the rest? You genuinely care about your customers. You genuinely care about your staff. You genuinely care about your vendors. Taking care of customers is not just being pleasant and friendly although that is important. It is also setting up processes and procedures that give your staff the ability to manage customer interactions the way you would but without you having to be there hovering over their shoulders.

Customer service is about making the process smooth and seamless. It is about removing the vexatious stumbling blocks to a quick and painless sale such as voicemail hell, onerous return policies, chatting help, endless transaction processes. .Make a list of all the things that you have experienced when you have had excellent customer service and a list of things you have experienced then you have had poor customer service.

Once you have created your list think about how you will avoid the negatives and how you will implement the positives for your own business. Set up a training program for you and your staff that will allow you to ensure that every customer who encounters anybody associated with your business will have the same level of satisfaction with your product everyone they know.

Use the Customer Response Process Map to guide you in creation of your customer service system. Be specific about how you will deal with your customers and how you will manage all of your interactions with them.

This system is the start of creating an entire customer service center that will allow you to train new employees and guide them toward understanding your business philosophy and how you want your customers to be treated.

Excellent Customer Service List:

1) _____

2) _____

3) _____

4) _____

5) _____

Poor Customer Service List

1) _____

2) _____

3) _____

4) _____

5) _____

Figure 34. List of Customer Service Experiences

Customer Response Process Map

- What is my Product?
- What is my USP?
- Who is my customer?
- What are the benefits of my product to my customers?
- Why should they care?
- How do I market my product to my customer?
- How do I provide my product to my customer?
- Who handles contacts with my customers?
- How do I greet potential customers?
- How many rings before the phone is answered?
- How long before emails are responded to?
- What is my phone script?
- How are customers treated when they arrive?
- What is my script for asking for referrals?
- What is my script for asking for repeat business?
- What is my sales staff dress code?
- What is my guarantee?
- How many products do I sell in a year?
- How many customers do I have?
- How many return customers do I have?
- How do I know people are happy with my product?
- How many complaints do I receive per year?
- What is my procedure for handling complaints?
- How do I turn complainers into advocates?
- How many customers return and buy again after a complaint?

Figure 35. Customer Response Process Map

Customer Complaints and Root Cause Analysis

Review your customer complaints. Rank them on a bar chart from most to least. Perform a root-cause analysis to find a way to eliminate the problem. Move on to the next one in order.

You don't know where you stand unless you measure it. Just as you get a report on your profitability every month you should be getting reports on how well your customers like your products and your service. If you rely on a few friends or a couple of complainers to drive your response you may end up far away from understanding the real issues your business faces.

How do you know which complaints to deal with? One tool is the Pareto Chart (Investopedia, n.d.) which allows you to visualize the complaints your receive as a histogram so you can decide which are the most important ones to tackle. Often we deal with the easiest complaints and leave the harder ones for later only to end up never dealing with them. By not dealing with them they crop up again and again.

The Pareto Chart helps you decide which issues have the most impact so you can deal with them in a systematic way. The chart stems from the Pareto Principle (Investopedia, n.d.) which is also known as the 80/20 rule. It states that 80% of your profits come from 20% of your customers. Or, in this case 80% of your customer complaints come from 20% of the issues.

> Here is an example of a Pareto chart ranking using Joe's customer complaints. He had numerous complaints the previous year. The top four totalled 48 costing him $15,000 to fix last year and 18 of them were due to poor workmanship on the part of his contractors. Poor workmanship accounted not only for the largest number of complaints but also well over 80% of the warranty cost in dollars he incurred.

Joe wants to reduce the frequency to prevent customers from becoming upset with him and to encourage them to come back and use him again. He also wants to reduce his warranty costs which average 3% of his gross revenues.

He tackles one problem at a time and takes on the one that happens most often which is poor workmanship. How will Joe deal with this situation? He could have a meeting with his craftsmen and tell them to do better work or else. That may or may not work. Instead, perhaps he should try to find the root cause of the problem.

Handyman Joe's Customer Complaints

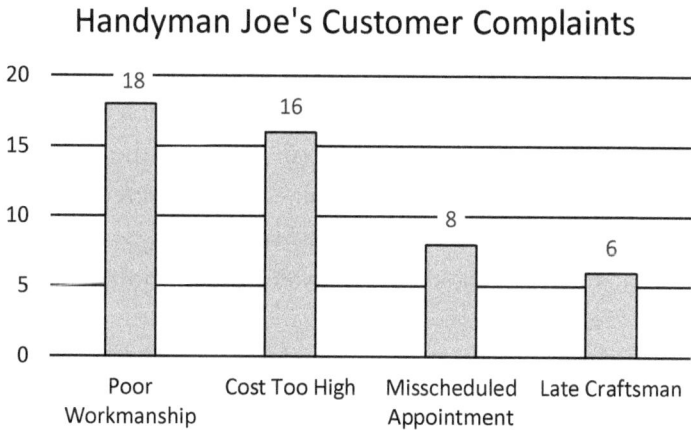

Figure 36. Customer Complaint Pareto Chart

Root cause analysis involves asking "Why?" You ask "Why?" over and over until you run out of "Why's" to ask. He could do this as a brainstorming session with his craftsmen and/or with his office staff. Why are Joe's customers complaining about poor workmanship? The obvious answer is that the craftsmen make mistakes.

But is that the root cause? Why do craftsmen make mistakes? It could be that they are incompetent. It could be that they are trying to cheat customers and make more money for doing work too fast and too cheap. As we have learned though, Joe has improved his hiring process dramatically so that is not a likely cause anymore.

Why do craftsmen make mistakes in their work? Assuming that they are reasonably competent and that they do want to do a good job for their customers and for Joe what other reasons could there be?

When Joe spent some time with his craftsmen, his office staff and his disgruntled customers a pattern emerged. Half of the problems were due to miscommunication between the craftsman and the customer.

In fact when Joe reviewed the contracts his craftsmen wrote out and compared them to the work that was completed there were many discrepancies. Those discrepancies were the source of sometimes major misunderstandings between the craftsmen and the customers.

Joe went back to his craftsmen and over several of his regular monthly meetings with them he conducted brainstorming sessions. In brainstorming you set up a flip chart and start asking for ideas. No idea is wrong or too far out. Everything gets recorded. Then the ideas get analyzed and the most likely ones are addressed further.

Joe asked, "Why?" over and over and found that often the craftsmen, a) did not see the need for written contracts and b) felt too rushed to write down a complete job. A detailed, step-by-step procedure might be:

Paint master bedroom, 10' x 12' x 8', prime walls first, add two coats flat robin's egg blue, ceiling painted flat white, one coat, doors not painted, trim painted two coats semigloss, closet not painted. Move furniture, use drop cloths throughout, put down crop cloths on carpeting from foyer to bedroom. Clean up and remove all trash.

Instead what was often written was:

Paint bedroom

What happened was that a customer might have a different color in mind or forget that the doors were not included in the price. Sometimes a customer would even change his mind after signing a contract trying to get the craftsmen to fix it for free. Suddenly the craftsman would have a dispute that often required Joe to mediate and cost him a lot of money to fix.

Joe now realized that it wasn't that the craftsmen were incompetent it was that they did not understand the need for a well-written contract. Now, instead of threatening to fire his staff he had something to train them on. His task now was to educate them on the importance of the contract and set performance goals to get them to change their habits.

Once his craftsmen understood the need to write better contracts and the benefits they would receive for taking a few more minutes of time up front the customer complaints dropped. He ended up with one craftsman who would not change and even though he otherwise performed well Joe let him go. He was costing the business too much money and too much goodwill with Joe's otherwise happy customers.

Now, after implementing the new procedure Joe's complaints dropped to 36. Just as important, his warranty costs dropped from $15,000 to $11,000 as his revenues were rising from $500,000 to $733,000.

His cost has now overtaken poor workmanship in number of complaints. All of the customer complaint issues are showing a decline just by virtue of the greater attention placed on handling customer complaints in general. Since cost is now a largest customer complaint factor that is the next item on the list to tackle.

Handyman Joe's Customer Complaints

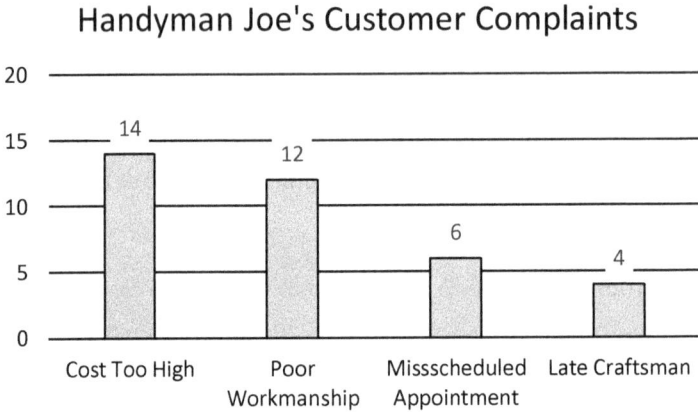

Figure 37. Customer Complaint Pareto Chart - After

Measuring Customer Satisfaction

How do you know when your customers are happy? How do you know what makes them happy or unhappy? By asking them. Few customers will lodge a complaint if you deliver poor service or product quality. Fewer still will tell you how well you did when you made them happy. Even if you have a written guarantee, very few people actually make use of it.

More and more businesses are aggressively trying to find out what their customers think of them. You see pop-up surveys on the internet even if you are just stopping by a website and haven't even used the product. Concepts such as KPIs – Key

Performance Indicators and Net Promoter Scores permeate marketers' talk.

You want to learn about:

<u>Customer satisfaction</u> – How did you like your service today?

<u>Customer loyalty</u> – Would you recommend this business to others?

<u>Importance of product attributes</u> – How satisfied are you with performance? How important is this to you?

<u>Intention to Return</u> – Would you buy more or again?

You can telephone, ask customers when they return to your store, use email or browser pop-ups. It is helpful to get a statistically significant number of responses and avoid asking people to answer who you know like your product. You want to find out how people actually feel so you can make changes as needed to your product and your sales and product support process. The more you know the better.

Net Promoter Score

Net promoter score involves asking customer to give a rank number out of 10 about their feelings about your product. For each of these questions you get a point score from 0 – 10. If you got a 9 or 10 that person is a Promoter. If you got a 7 or 8 that person is a Passive and 6 or below are Detractors.

Compile the percentage who are Promoters and subtract the percentage who are Detractors. The result is your NPS. If you can find scores of competitors asking the same questions you can compare yourself. If you take this survey over time you can see if you are getting better or worse.

Those who score 9 or 10 are people who like you so much that they will refer others to you. These are your evangelists.

143

If they are below 7 they are people who will tell others not to do business with you. This is a simple way to figure out where you stand. You certainly hope that there are more customers promoting you than saying bad things about you.

The main point is that you need to communicate with your customers constantly to ensure that you are providing a product and the service to go along with it that they appreciate. Your customers can be a great source of innovation and ideas for improvement.

See customer complaints as a gift rather than a negative. If customers don't care about you they won't say anything. If they care enough to complain that means they like you and want you to do better by them. Customer complaints are an opportunity to turn a Detractor into a Promoter depending on how well you deal with the complaint.

Net Promoter Score Questions

- How happy are you with our speed and efficiency?
- How happy are you with our attention to your needs?
- How happy are you with the way we answered your questions and gave you recommendations?
- How satisfied are you overall with us?
- How would you feel about recommending us to your friends?

Figure 38. Net Promoter Score

Chapter 8

Profit Margin

Profit margin, as we discussed in Chapter 2, is the amount of money left over after the expenses are paid divided by the money your customers pay you for your products. It is a measure of efficiency of your operation because if you reduce your expenses you have greater profit margin which means more money in your pocket, and sadly, vice versa.

You can use profit margin as a tool for comparing your business from one time period to the next, for future planning and to compare your business to others.

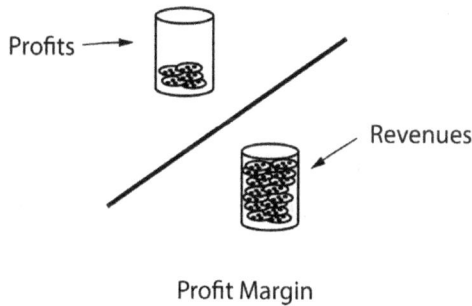

Profits →

Revenues ←

Profit Margin

Figure 39. Profit Margin

In our 5-Part Process Profit Margin is the filter for all the hard work you do to run your business. You do Prospecting, getting people to know about your business and interested in buying from you. You sell your product, Converting your Prospects into Customers. You determine your Price and your customer service level determines how many times Customers Return. The Profit Margin reflects the ease or difficulty you have making money with your system.

Each part of the 5 Part Process affects your profitability. You may be tempted to spend a lot of money to gain prospects through marketing efforts. You may feel uncomfortable asking your customers for referrals or asking them to come back and buy again. You may have spent your precious time trying to be nice to customers who don't care about your product, who just want to demand the lowest price.

We have seen how sometimes small changes can create large results for the amount of profits you earn. Let's look at each of the parts of profit and see how the work separately.

When you look at your P&L you see that there are several kinds of profit. The first is gross profit or operating profit. This is what is left over after you take out your expenses for producing and selling your product. These expenses are your Variable Cost. Variable Cost is the amount of money that goes into making each specific item or service that is sold.

If you sell a widget such as a car or a pen or a sock monkey you are making an individual item. All of the raw materials you buy to make the pen or car are variable costs, so-named because the total amount you spend varies with how many you produce. If you make ten pens it costs ten times the amount of plastic and metal and ink than it would take to make one pen.

The Cost of Goods Sold or your Variable Costs are the costs that go into the actual creation of the product or service. If you are making sock monkeys that would be the cost of the socks and felt and thread and googly eyeballs and the labor it takes to sew up your sock monkeys.

Also, if you have a production plant to make sock monkeys the amount of labor used to make them will vary with the number produced as well. If you make 10 sock monkeys per week in your home you might be making them by yourself. When your business expands and you get orders for 100 sock monkeys per week you might then have to hire 10 people to make them, each person making 10 sock monkeys per week.

After accounting for your Variable Costs you still have Fixed Costs to consider. Fixed Costs are office rent, administrative staff, sometimes sales staff; any cost that does not depend on the number of products sold. If you rent an office space the amount of rent you pay is the same from month-to-month regardless whether you make 40 sock monkeys per month or 4,000. After accounting for your Fixed Costs you are left with Net Profit Before Taxes. Another term for this is EBITDA or Earnings Before Interest, Taxes, Depreciation and Amortization.

This is the number corporations usually report as their Profit. After you pay your taxes and take into account interest paid on loans to the company and account for depreciation of your assets you are left with your actual dollars of profit in your pocket. In this book we will talk about EBITDA when we say Profit or Net Profit.

Breaking Even

One of the key numbers to know for a business is its Breakeven Point. This is the point where you actually start to earn a profit. It is the point where you change over from just paying bills to having extra cookies in your cookie jar.

Every month you need to generate enough money to pay for your overhead. Once that point is reached you start earning profits. Every time you incur an extra cost you push back the day of the month you start to earn a profit.

Let's look at a simplified Profit & Loss report for Handyman Joe's business:

> For Joe's business this is the cost of the contractors who make 50% of the Total Revenues for their jobs. It includes

the royalties Joe pays since that is a percentage of the gross profit as well. His warranty costs end up being a percentage of the revenues. All together just over 2/3's of his revenues go to pay for making his product. His product is the service he provides for his customers, repairing their homes. The total amount he spends for his Variable Costs depends on how many sales he makes.

Handyman Joe's
Profit & Loss 2013

Prospects	2,000	
Conversion Rate	50%	
Number of Customers	1,000	
Average Revenue per Customer	$500	
Total Revenues	$ 500,000	
Manufacturing Costs (Variable Costs)		
Total Variable Costs	$ 340,000	68%
Gross Profits	$ 160,000	32%
Overhead Costs (Fixed Costs)		
Total Fixed Costs	$ 130,000	26%
Net Profit Before Taxes	$30,000	
Average Profit Per Customer	$30	
Profit Margin	6%	

Figure 40. Handyman Joe's Results for 2013

His Overhead or Fixed Costs are costs that are nearly always the same from month to month. Costs such are his storefront rent and utilities, internet and telephone and the cost of his office staff. This cost is $130,000 per year. This means Joe has to take in $10,333 every month no matter how much or how little he sells to pay for these expenses.

At what point does Handyman Joe actually start putting cookies <u>into</u> his cookie jar? For every dollar he earns in revenues 68¢ goes right back out to pay for his product cost – his Variable Costs. The remaining 32¢ goes to pay off the $10,333 for the monthly Overhead or Fixed Costs until the bills are paid.

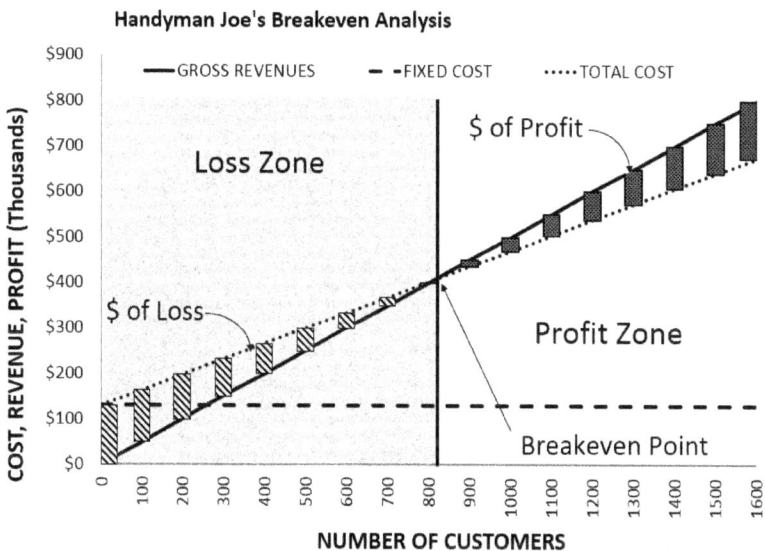

Handyman Joe's Breakeven Analysis

Figure 41. Handyman Joe's Breakeven Analysis

Don't forget that bills are "lumpy." Some bills are paid immediately, some in a month or two, some are annual or quarterly such as income & sales taxes or workmen's comp insurance. So, one month Joe may pay out $20,000 in fixed costs and the next $6,000.

The Breakeven Point is the place where Revenues equal Total Costs summing to zero. The very next product sold allows you to put some cookies (cookie crumbs actually) in your company cookie jar. We can graph the result of accumulating sales and see where the Breakeven Point is using a relatively simple formula. The Breakeven Point is expressed as the number of products sold.

> The breakeven analysis shows how many sales you have to make before profits start to appear. The dashed horizontal line across the bottom of the graph above represents Joe's fixed costs at $130,000 per year. The dotted line that starts at $130,000 along with the fixed cost line is the total of the fixed and variable costs. This grows as you move right along the graph because the total cost to make the product keeps getting larger as the number of customers served grows.

The solid line starting at zero is the Gross Revenues and as long as it is below the Total Cost line profits are in the negative zone (you are losing money). The point where Gross Revenues equals Total Cost gives you the number of products you have to sell, in this case the number of customers served, so your revenues equal your expenses.

 Once you pass that point you are in the Profit Zone and every sale you make after that earns you profit. In this case a profit of 38 cents of every dollar in sales

> The breakeven point for Joe is actually 812 customers for the year. With $500,000 in sales and 1,000 customers, Joe is just beyond his breakeven point as we have seen earlier. It is only his last 190 customers of the year who earn him his $30,000 profit. Every sale that happens before just pays the bills.

This also shows why profits can build up or fall off quickly because once Joe's overhead costs are paid for any extra sale is profitable.

For example, if Handyman Joe generates an additional $100,000 in sales it earns him an additional $38,000 in profits since the fixed cost overhead has already been paid off for the year.

But I'm sure at this point you are saying, that's just that one business. I don't run a construction operation, I make and sell sock monkeys or I am a realtor or I am a business consultant or I sell phone apps. The -principles are all the same, although the numbers will be different – each business has its unique proportion of fixed and variable costs.

Here is another example:

My son, Colby, wanted to go on a school trip to Europe and his goal was to personally earn $1,000 toward the trip above and beyond the school fundraisers he had to participate in to fund it. His idea was to bag and sell candy to his schoolmates between classes. He was going to add 10% to the cost of the candy and bag as his profit.

His profit goal was thus $1,000. His business model was quite simple: he had no overhead – no fixed costs as he was not paying for rent or utilities. He would fill the baggies himself for no pay keeping his variable costs down. He and I would buy the candy at discount bulk stores and he was to reimburse me for the cost from his sales (essentially a zero interest loan). He would then put 88 cents worth of candy into a bag that costs 2 cents each – his variable cost totalling 90 cents.

When we look at his Proforma Profit & Loss Statement (A Pro-Forma is a monetary projection looking into the future) we find problems with this approach:

	10% Profit
Revenues	$ 10,000
Variable Costs	
Materials & Labor	$ 9,000
Gross Profit	$ 1,000
Fixed Costs	
Overhead	$ -
Net Profit	$ 1,000
# of Customers	10,000
Revenue per Customer	$ 1.00

Figure 42. Colby's Candy Business Profitability

Since he has zero fixed costs he is making a profit from the very first sale. But it is a pretty teensy profit. He will have to make 10,000 sales to earn his $1,000 of profit. To do this in one year he would have to make 27 sales per day every single day of the year. Doesn't sound very feasible unfortunately.

What if he increased his prices? Selling the candy at $1.50 each gives him a 40% profit margin. Now has to make "only" 1,755 sales to earn his $1,000. If his price is $2.00 each it will take 943 sales which is still 2.5 sales per day for a year.

The question now is could he even sell his candy bags for $2 each? These are candy bags that sell for about a dollar at the cafeteria at his school. Would the convenience of candy delivery give him the ability to name his price? He could conduct a survey of his potential customers and ask how much they would be willing to pay as a starting point for developing his price strategy.

By doubling his price he would reduce the number of sales necessary to reach his goal by a factor of 5 from 10,000 to 943.

	10% Profit	40% Profit	55% Profit
Revenues	$ 10,000	$ 2,633	$ 1,886
Variable Costs			
Materials & Labor	$ 9,000	$ 1,632	$ 886
Gross Profit	$ 1,000	$ 1,000	$ 1,000
Fixed Costs			
Overhead	$ -	$ -	$ -
Net Profit	$ 1,000	$ 1,000	$ 1,000
# of Customers	10,000	1,755	943
Revenue per Customer	$ 1.00	$ 1.50	$ 2.00

Figure 43. Colby's Candy Business Profitability Revised

Now, look at your own business. On the next page is the formula to calculate breakeven point and a form to use to calculate it. I want you to use either method for your business: How close are your business results to the number you calculate? If you are well above this then you should be making some decent profits from your business.

To use either the equation or the calculation you need to know the Variable Cost per Item. If you know that number already you can skip step 6 and just insert it in place of the term 5) VC / I. If you don't know it then you can calculate it in step six by dividing your total Variable Cost by the number of units you made or services performed

Number of Sales =	Fixed Costs
	(Selling Price – Variable Cost Per Item)

Figure 44. Breakeven Formula

How to Calculate Your Breakeven Point:

1) Fixed Costs (FC) = _____
   How much do you spend on overhead, rent, computer, phone, office supplies, office personnel?

2) Variable Costs (VC) = _____
   How much do you spend on raw materials, wages for making your product, sales commissions, advertising traceable to specific sales?

3) Selling Price (P) = _____
   How much do you sell your product for?

4) Number of Items (I) = _____
   How many items do you make for the amount of money you spend on your variable costs?

5) Calculate Variable Cost per Item
   = 2) / 4) = VC / I = _____

6) Subtract 5) from 3) = P – VC / I = _____

7) Divide 1) by 6) = FC / (P – VC / I) = _____

   This is the number of items you need to sell at the price you are charging to reach your breakeven point.

Figure 45. Calculating Breakeven Point

Profit Margin and Efficiency

Profit Margin is a measure of how efficiently your business is run. When you look at your monthly performance results you can see if your profit margin has increased or decreased. Your dollars of profit may change but the ratio of profits to revenues tells you how well or poorly you spent your money.

At first, as your business grows you will see your profit margin increase as your revenues grow while your fixed costs stay the same. When you expand, moving into a storefront or hiring personnel your profit margin will drop until you incorporate them into your business and these new resources start contributing to your profits.

As you add staffing positions there needs to be enough work to justify them. As the owner, ideally, you should only create those positions you have worked yourself and understand well enough to carve off your responsibility to someone else.

When you prepare to hire your first employee think about how you will be able to train and promote her down the road. How can you generate and keep her loyal to you and your company in this era of constant job flipping?

You want to have a reasonably happy workforce eager to do a good job for you and have people with good people skills managing them. Having a disgruntled workforce makes it very difficult to provide superlative customer service. You want to create a nurturing corporate culture and fill it with self-actuated people to be successful.

In the daily chaos of running our businesses we often get wrapped up in everyday operations and forget to stop and look around to see if we are still heading in the right direction.

Looking at your monthly results, your P&L, your Profit Margin, and other reports let you see if you are on track when you compare them to your previous months' results. You can even compare your business with your competitors' (if you can get their numbers).

If your profit margin is lower than your competitor's then perhaps you are not finding the lowest cost raw materials supplier. Or perhaps it means they are buying lower quality raw materials and your product has better quality characteristics allowing you to raise prices.

You cannot compare profit margin between unrelated businesses as each type of operation has a different financial makeup. Grocery stores have very low profit margins and can't be compared to luxury products like Rolex watches which have an extremely high markup.

Profit margin is a tool you can use to monitor the health of your business and it is a knob you can turn to improve your business as well.

If your profit margin is 10% you have to earn $10 in revenues for every $1 of profit you make. That means that if you need to buy a $1000 laptop you have to bring in $10,000 extra in revenues to your business or your profits and your profit margin will drop. Even at a 50% profit margin that $1000 laptop requires $2,000 in revenues.

> Since Handyman Joe's net profit margin for his handyman business was 6% it costs him $16,667 in revenues to pay for that new $1,000 laptop if he wants to keep his current $30,000 annual profits. Otherwise profits drop by $1,000 down to $29,000.

You may need to entertain clients or do extensive networking to promote your business. Don't skimp on spending money to make money. Be aware of the dividing line between spending for your business and spending used as an excuse for playing golf, buying fancy office equipment or hiring lots of people. Be ruthless with your expenses.

Now that you know how to measure your profits and profit margin you will know where you stand financially. In the rest of this book we will manipulate the factors controlling profits and profit margin to turn our businesses into Profit Machines.

Return on Investment

Whenever you make an investment in your business you should be able to justify it monetarily. The way to measure the value your investment returns is through Return on Investment, abbreviated, ROI. The ROI is the amount of profits earned as a result of this cost.

When you hire a new employee you should be able to operate your business more efficiently and earn more money; otherwise you will quickly go broke. If you increase your marketing spending you should earn more money by increasing the number of prospects in your sales funnel.

> Handyman Joe tried marketing his business in two different locations in his franchise area that he had not spent much effort on in the past. He spent $1,000 to drop 7,500 flyers at selected portal walks in the Northeast part of his territory and another $1,000 for four display ads in a local free weekly paper in the Southwest part.
>
> His goal was to test the effectiveness of his marketing and to determine how well display ads work compared to flyers. Both target areas have similar demographics.
>
> Over the next month he received 100 phone calls from the traditional flyers dropped in the Northeast for 55

signed contracts and $25,000 in business and $1,500 profits – a 50% ROI ($1,500 profits – the $1,000 cost of the flyers) = $500 divided by the $1,000 cost of the flyers).

His display ads generated 25 phone calls and 10 signed contracts for $4,500 in sales and $270 in profits for a – 73% ROI ($270 in profits - $1,000 cost of ads) = - $730 / $1,000 cost of the ads).

Before he started using ROI to analyze his marketing spending Joe would have continued with his spending on display ads. Since he earned more revenues and more customers he would have felt it worthwhile.

But the display ads did not generate more profits. After taking into account the cost of his advertising by calculating his ROI, he was actually operating at a loss. If he kept on doing this kind of marketing he would eventually go out of business.

Although display advertisements had been effective in the past they have become less and less effective over time. The same was occurring with yellow pages advertising since people have mostly stopped using the telephone book to look up phone numbers and addresses.

Synergies Between the 5 Parts of Profit

The interesting thing about profit margin is that if you make the other four parts of profit work for you your profit margin itself improves as a result of making those improvements.

If you can increase the number of prospects in your sales funnel without spending more money on marketing, your marketing costs are spread out over more people and your profit margin increases. One way to increase prospects in your sales funnel is through referral programs which can be less expensive than advertisements.

As your conversion rate improves you are making more efficient use of your existing prospects in your sales funnel so your marketing and sales costs decrease meaning your profit margin improves.

If you increase prices things are a bit more complex. The law of supply and demand says that if you increase prices your volume drops as fewer customers will buy at a higher price.

However, the economic concept called elasticity of supply and demand which says that there is a certain amount of "stickiness" to your clientele. This means they won't just automatically leave you if prices rise – up to a certain point of course.

This elasticity is demonstrated by gasoline prices. I'm sure you have noticed that prices jump up very quickly whenever there is a jiggle in the worldwide supply but it seems to take much longer to drop back down. There are a number of reasons for that but you can take advantage of the effect with your prices and the demand that your customers have for your products.

You have some leeway with your good customers. If you lose those customers who are detractors you may actually be better off. How much time do you spend trying to deal with a customer who has paid the minimum price for a product and is complaining all the time compared to taking care of your best customers? By concentrating on your good customers and thus generating greater loyalty from them you earn more repeat business and referrals.

Too low of a price can be as bad as too high. If your price is too low then at best you are not taking in as much money as you could and in fact you could be telling customers that your product is not just cheap but also chintzy – that you are selling them the low-quality mass-market version. By making your customers feel proud to own your product they will be willing to pay more for it.

When you do a better job of training your personnel in handling customers, customer service levels improve and you can expect to have more customers come back more often. Increasing the number of customers again increases your profit margin.

Putting The Five Parts of Profit To Work

Using an example of Handyman Joe's Profit & Loss Statement we will go through the Five Parts of Profit and the effect that incremental changes have on his profits. We have seen what happened when he individually improved each part. Now we will see what happens when each part changes along with the others.

On this page and the next are charts showing how expenses and profits change when Handyman Joe's business changes. By focusing on each of the 5 Parts of Profit he completely changed his business, turning it into a Profit Machine.

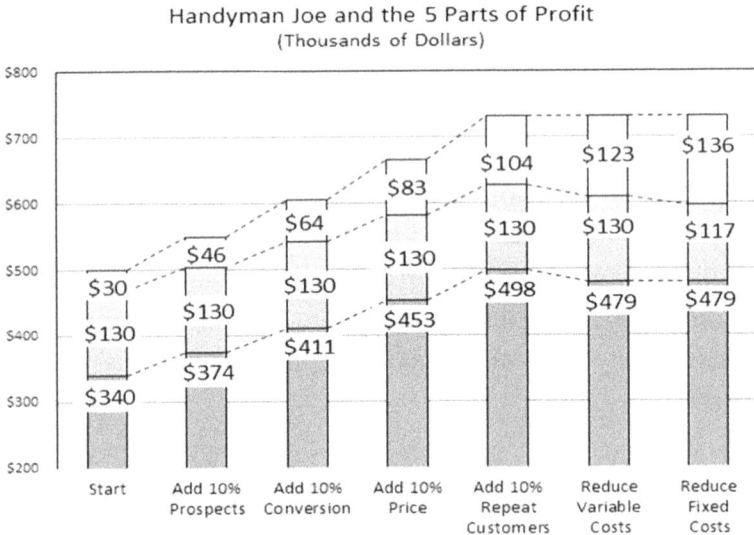

Handyman Joe and the 5 Parts of Profit
(Thousands of Dollars)

	Start	Add 10% Prospects	Add 10% Conversion	Add 10% Price	Add 10% Repeat Customers	Reduce Variable Costs	Reduce Fixed Costs
Top	$30	$46	$64	$83	$104	$123	$136
Middle	$130	$130	$130	$130	$130	$130	$117
Bottom	$130	$130	$130	$453	$498	$479	$479
	$340	$374	$411				

Figure 46. Putting the 5 Parts of Profit to Work

Handyman Joe's Profit & Loss 2013	Start	Add 10% Prospects	Add 10% Conversion	Add 10% Price	Add 10% Repeat	Reduce Variable	Reduce Fixed Costs
Prospects	2,000	2,200	2,200	2,200	2,200	2,200	2,200
Conversion Rate	50%	50%	55%	55%	55%	55%	55%
Number of Customers	1,000	1,100	1,210	1,210	1,210	1,210	1,210
Price	$500	$500	$500	$550	$550	$550	$550
Repeat Customers	1.0	1.0	1.0	1.0	1.1	1.1	1.1
Total Revenues	$ 500,000	$ 550,000	$ 605,000	$ 665,500	$ 732,050	$ 732,050	$ 732,050
Manufacturing Costs (Variable Costs)	$ 340,000	$ 374,000	$ 411,400	$ 452,540	$ 497,794	$ 479,493	$ 479,493
Gross Profits	$ 160,000	$ 176,000	$ 193,600	$ 212,960	$ 234,256	$ 252,557	$ 252,557
Overhead Costs (Fixed Costs)	$ 130,000	$ 130,000	$ 130,000	$ 130,000	$ 130,000	$ 130,000	$ 117,000
Net Profit	$30,000	$46,000	$63,600	$82,960	$104,256	$122,557	$135,557
Average Profit Per Customer	$30	$42	$53	$69	$86	$101	$112
Profit Margin	6%	8%	11%	12%	14%	17%	19%

Figure 47. Improving the 5 Parts of Profit - Spreadsheet

You can see how the small, 10% changes Joe made to his operation more than quadrupled his profits in six incremental steps. Joe initially thought he would have to quadruple his number of customers to quadruple his profits but by concentrating on different aspects of his business he found that the smaller changes he made had much larger results than he imagined.

Now, let's look in greater detail what happens with these incremental 10% changes.

Increasing Prospective Customers 10%

Assume Handyman Joe increases his Marketing spending by 10% to promote his business. This means he has another 200 possible customers in his sales funnel. He could have accomplished this through improving his referral business or by sending out more flyers. To be conservative we will assume that his referral program costs as much as sending out flyers. If it was less expensive he would end up with an even better result by virtue of lowering his variable costs.

	Start	Increase Prospects 10%
Number of Prospects	2,000	2,200
Conversion Rate	50%	50%
# of Customers	1,000	1,100
Price	$500	$500
# of Repeat Customers	1	1
Profit Margin	6.0%	8.4%
Profits	$ 30,000	$ 46,000

Figure 48. Increase Number of Prospects by 10%

Generating another 200 Prospective Customers means that at his current 50% Conversion Rate he has earned an additional 100 Customers. To do this requires spending another $34,000 in his Marketing to earn an additional $50,000 in Revenues.

Because he is already past his breakeven point he has paid off his Fixed Costs and the remaining $16,000 is Profit. Because of these additional Profits his Profit Margin has also increased from 6% to 8% which 1/3 more than he started with.

Increasing Conversion Rate by 10%

The next step is to increase the rate he Converts Prospects into Customers by 10%. Assume Joe has already improved his Marketing as we saw above.

Joe worked to improve the sales skills of his office staff and his craftsmen. Through the use of scripts, better hiring practices and better training his craftsmen were functioning more efficiently in generating more sales. They spent less time looking for new work so their earnings improved. In turn their morale shot up which helped them win even more jobs. Now Joe's Conversion Rate has improved from 50% to 55%.

	Increase Prospects 10%	Increase Conversion Rate by 10%
Number of Prospects	2,200	2,200
Conversion Rate	50%	55%
# of Customers	1,100	1,210
Price	$500	$500
# of Repeat Customers	1	1
Profit Margin	8.4%	10.5%
Profits	$ 46,000	$ 63,600

Figure 49. Increase Conversion Rate 10%

As a result his Revenues improved by $55,000 and his Net Profit more than doubled from the initial $30,000 to $63,000. He still has 2,200 Prospects in his sales funnel but now he has an additional 110 Customers and his Profit Margin is now 11% which is almost double what he started with.

Increasing Price

To increase his prices Joe could raise his internal billing rate from $100/hr. to $110/hr but he already knows from experience that this would be counterproductive. Price is already an issue he has to be very careful about. Raising his billing rates any further could price him out of the market entirely.

	Increase Conversion Rate by 10%	Increase Price by 10%
Number of Prospects	2,200	2,200
Conversion Rate	55%	55%
# of Customers	1,210	1,210
Price	$500	$550
# of Repeat Customers	1	1
Profit Margin	10.5%	12.5%
Profits	$ 63,600	$ 82,960

Figure 50. Increase Price 10%

But through Joe's improved training procedures his craftsmen and his office staff have learned a lot about sales and selling. In addition to closing more sales thereby increasing Joe's Conversion Rate they are actually closing more work per sale improving his Price.

This is a result of asking customers "What Else?" while pricing jobs with customers. In effect he has raised his Price by getting more work per customers every time he signs a contract. He could try bundling different services together or offering annual home maintenance contracts as well.

Now Joe's average sale is $550 instead of $500. An extra $50 per customer from his 1,210 customers means an additional $60,500 in Revenues almost $53,000 of which are pure Profit. Profits are now $82,960 from the starting $30,000 for a Profit Margin of 12%.

Increasing the Number of Repeat Customers

Joe has been having his staff call each customer after every job has been completed to find out how the work went. This gives him valuable information about how well or how poorly his craftsmen have performed, how well the work went and to ask customers for more work.

	Increase Price by 10%	Increase Repeat Customers by 10%
Number of Prospects	2,200	2,200
Conversion Rate	55%	55%
# of Customers	1,210	1,210
Price	$550	$550
# of Repeat Customers	1	1.1
Profit Margin	12.5%	14.2%
Profits	$ 82,960	$ 104,256

Figure 51. Increase Repeat Customers 10%

His computerized Customer Relationship Management (CRM) program keeps track of extra jobs his customers bring up during the bidding process with the craftsmen. The office staff calls the customers when they anticipate doing the next home improvement project on their list to try to generate more work.

By transforming his office into a customer-service oriented operation Customer Value has now increased 10% from $550 to $605 due to repeat business thus earning an additional $67,000 in revenues.

Note that this is a conservative estimate as we are assuming Joe has not increased the number of Customers and that his customer referral business costs as much as his marketing for new customers. His Profits are now over $100,000 and the Profit Margin is up to 14%

Increasing Profit Margin

Joe's Profit Margin has improved from 6% to 14% by virtue of incremental improvement in the four Revenue parts of his business. What happens when he works specifically on his efficiency?

Reducing Variable Costs

What if Joe works to reduce his Variable Costs? Variable Costs include the amount he pays his craftsmen for doing the work. It is set at 50% as part of the way the franchise operates. If he were to reduce that he would have problems attracting and keeping the quality of craftsman he has so he is not going to try to change that.

He cannot change his Royalty payments. If anything they will rise the next time his franchise contract expires but that won't happen for several more years.

	Increase Repeat Customers by 10%	Increase Profit Margin - Reduce Variable Costs
Number of Prospects	2,200	2,200
Conversion Rate	55%	55%
# of Customers	1,210	1,210
Price	$550	$550
# of Repeat Customers	1.1	1.1
Profit Margin	14.2%	16.7%
Profits	$ 104,256	$ 122,557

Figure 52. Reducing Variable Costs

Joe felt that his Warranty costs were too high. These costs have traditionally been at 3% of his gross revenues – at $500,000 revenues this means he paid $15,000 to repair problems resulting from poor workmanship and customer complaints not covered by his insurance.

With the work he has done to improve hiring and training and customer follow-up and his use of the Pareto Chart to identify customer complaint issues Joe cuts his rate of Warranty repairs in half and it now stands at 1.5%.

When his greater revenues are factored in it would have gone up to $22,000 if he had made no improvements. Now, it still costs him $11,000 per year to fix his mistakes so he will continue to work on that issue.

What if Joe was able to reduce his Advertising cost from 10% to 9%? Since he is better at Prospecting and Conversion he should be more efficient at getting customers to sign contracts so he can reduce spending there. His repeat customer and referral programs allow him to spend less money to obtain new customers and this is where it will show up – in reduced marketing and advertising cost. Alternatively, he could maintain his Advertising rates to drive even more business to his door if he has the ability to serve the larger number of customers.

At this point his Revenues have increased by almost 50%. He has to bring on an additional 4 or 5 craftsmen to take up the extra workload. This does not change his variable cost percentage because they are paid based on the amount of revenues they bring in.

At some point, though, he will also have to add office staff to handle the extra workload of handling the call volumen and dispatching and taking the bids from the craftsmen. This will reduce increase his Fixed Costs and at least temporarily reduce his Profit Margin.

His Variable Costs have now dropped to 66.5% from 68%. This means Variable Costs decrease by $18,000 and Profits increase by the same amount since his Fixed Costs remain the same. His Profit Margin has now increased an additional 3% to a total of 17%..

Reducing Fixed Costs

Now Joe works to reduce his Fixed Costs. A 10% reduction from $130,000 to $117,000 increases his Profits by the same $13,000. How did Joe accomplish this? By combing through his expenses he found a better and less expensive phone and Internet provider. He moved his office from a storefront to a back office area that was less expensive and still provided a meeting place for him and his craftsmen.

Joe is now generating over $120,000 in Profits up from the initial $30,000, 4 times what he started with. Joe has turned his business into a Profit Machine.

	Increase Profit Margin - Reduce Variable Costs	Increase Profit Margin - Reduce Fixed Costs
Number of Prospects	2,200	2,200
Conversion Rate	55%	55%
# of Customers	1,210	1,210
Price	$550	$550
# of Repeat Customers	1.1	1.1
Profit Margin	16.7%	18.5%
Profits	$ 122,557	$ 135,557

Figure 53. Reducing Fixed Costs

Of course as Joe keeps on expanding he will have to hire on more help. He may have to move his office to a larger space. His Fixed Expenses will increase but as long as he has them covered by increasing his revenues he can maintain his Profit Margin. Another issue is that as word gets out of Joe's success he will have more competitors. Other national franchises may test the waters in his area. He may have other craftsmen competing harder on price and will lose work due to that.

But if he continues the course he has set for himself and his business. If he keeps developing his craftsmen and office staff as a team he can remain ahead of his competitors and he can earn the profits he wants to generate the lifestyle he wants for himself and his family.

Chapter 9

Conclusion

There are five components to Profit. Each of these components represents a piece of what it takes to run a business. The underlying meaning of each part provides an aspect of business operations you can manipulate. Each component also has a numerical value that represents a real measure of how the business is performing.

When you multiply these five numerical values together you end up with the dollar amount of profit you earn for your business. In the examples used in this book the changes were small in order to demonstrate that it is feasible to generate drastically improved results without requiring drastically large changes. It is within the power of any of us to make these changes.

By understanding these Parts of Profit and learning how to control them your profit margin and your overall dollars of profit improve. A systematic approach to incremental and repeated improvements will transform your business into a profit-making machine.

Now it is your turn. Take your business in hand. Use the formulas, forms and examples from this book and dissect it into its own 5 Parts of Profit. Examine each of them in turn. Determine your ultimate business and personal goals and make sure they mesh. Now manipulate your 5 Parts of Profit to make your business meet and exceed your goals.

If your operation is doing what you want and you are making the money you need then that's OK. Just be careful of complacency. Maintaining the status quo often ends up as a slow decline. If you are not satisfied with your business and what it is doing then you have the opportunity to grab it by the scruff of its neck and shake it and transform it into the business you want.

You do this by creating a business designed for the next level or even the level beyond that then making continuous incremental changes to generate profit. You will have built a Profit Machine.

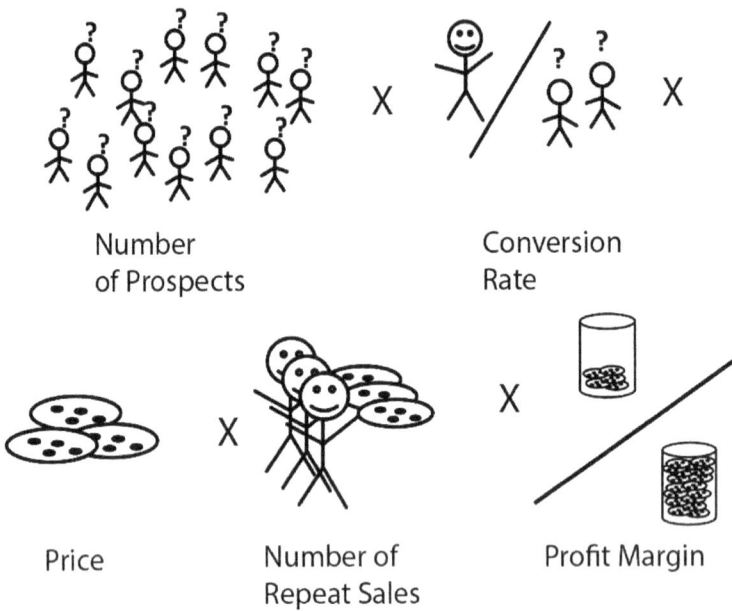

Number
of Prospects

Conversion
Rate

Price

Number of
Repeat Sales

Profit Margin

Figure 54. The Five Parts of Profit

Appendix

Handyman Joe's Handyman Franchise

Handyman Joe has a dozen craftsmen working for him performing the repair and renovation work at his customers' homes. On average they bring in about $4,000 or so per month each in gross revenues to the business and take half of those revenues for their compensation.

Joe's business took in $500,000 in revenues the previous year. The table below summarizes his profit & loss statement (this is adapted from a real-life example).

Joe's Cost of Goods Sold or Variable Costs are made up of his Contractor Costs which are 50% of the gross revenues. As a franchisee he pays out 5% of his gross earnings as royalties to the franchisor in return for the franchise system and national branding.

He ends up with about 3% in warranty repair costs from mistakes his craftsmen make and he is paying out 10% of his gross revenues in advertising. All this totals $340,000 equalling 68% of his revenues.

Variable Costs are called variable because they are proportional to the number of sales you make. Usually they are manufacturing costs (if you make an actual product) – the raw materials and labor that go into making a widget depends on the number of widgets.

If you make a widget and costing $1 for raw materials the raw material cost will be $1,000 to make 1,000 widgets and

$100,000 to make 100,000 widgets. Hence, the term variable.

The franchisors and the franchisees have found that in this business if they want more sales they increase the number of flyers they send out to the public and the response rate is fairly predictable.

Handyman Joe's Profit & Loss 2013

Prospects	2,000	
Conversion Rate	50%	
Number of Customers	1,000	
Average Customer Revenue	$500	
Total Revenues	$ 500,000	
Manufacturing Costs (Variable Costs)		
Contractor Costs	$ 250,000	50%
Customer Warranty Expense	$ 15,000	3.0%
Royalties	$ 25,000	5%
Advertising	$ 50,000	10%
Total Variable Costs	$ 340,000	68%
Gross Profits	$ 160,000	32%
Overhead Costs (Fixed Costs)		
Staff	$ 35,000	7%
Office Expenses	$ 60,000	12%
Marketing	$ 35,000	2%
Total Fixed Costs	$ 130,000	26%
Net Profit Before Taxes	$30,000	6%
Average Customer Profit	$30	
Profit Margin	6%	

Figure 55. Handyman Joe's P&L

This makes advertising cost to be more of a variable cost than fixed. For your own purposes categorize line items where they make the most sense for your business purposes. This may be different than what is done for tax purposes and that's OK. Set up reports for your needs to clarify your understanding of your business.

With the variable costs totalling $340,000 this leaves him $160,000 to pay for all his remaining expenses plus his salary & profit. His overhead or fixed costs are $130,000.

Fixed Costs mean that they do not change even though there are different numbers of products sold. No matter how much work Joe does for his customers his rent stays the same. So does his phone bill, internet bill and personnel cost (unless he hires someone or lays someone off).

That is why it is called Fixed Cost. Fixed and Variable Cost are concepts used to understand the cost structure of a business, where the breakeven point is and how to generate more profit.

With all that Joe has a before-tax profit of $30,000. His business is in the 20% tax bracket so he ends up paying $6,000 in taxes and has a net profit of $24,000.

This means that his reward for working 60 hour weeks trying to get customers to commit to his business, hiring (and firing) craftsmen, marketing his business, answering phones, doing bookkeeping, organizing stacks of flyers and taking them to the post office, and cleaning the office he is earning $8hr.

When you are starting a business this is called "Sweat Equity." Sweat Equity is the labor you perform unpaid and unacknowledged to build your business up from scratch. Once you reach a certain size you hire staff to take over some of those chores you do to save money such as bookkeeping, answering phones, vacuuming and cleaning the toilets.

Joe spent $60,000 out of his RRSP (he is in Canada – it would be his 401k in the U.S.) to buy the business. In Canada that $60,000 taken out of his retirement account was what was left over after he paid his taxes on the money. In the U.S he would have paid taxes plus suffered a 10% penalty for early withdrawal as well.

Joe also has a 5-year carry-back loan with the former owner for another $60,000. That loan costs him $13,500 a year from his earnings at a 5% interest rate. Now he has only $10,500 left to pay his mortgage and feed his family out of the remainder of his profits.

This is how many small businesses start. At the level of profit Joe is earning a small disaster can send him quickly into the red and turn his dream into bankruptcy.

Let's look more closely at one area Joe can try to make some improvements. His warranty costs have been averaging 3% of his gross revenues year after year. The warranty cost is due to Joe's craftsmen not being perfect. Even though he uses written contracts to minimize misunderstandings they still make mistakes. They use the wrong color paint or wrong type of wood. The customer changes her mind but insists the craftsman erred, etc.

Joe does have insurance (with a $1,000 deductible) but it doesn't make sense to use it for every issue that comes up. He had a plumber cause a flood in a customer's home during a $300 job that cost over $10,000 to repair. That was where the insurance was necessary. His rates went up the next year and he will end up paying the insurance company back over time for the repairs.

Now suppose he has a series of customer warranty problems due to poor workmanship costing him $5,000 to fix which isn't covered by his insurance. Now his profits are down to $5,500. Or his franchise contract is due for renewal and now his royalties are 7% instead of 5% - there goes another $10,000 per year right out of his profits.

At this point why is Joe in this business? Does he hope things will get better? Is it that the economy is bad? Is it that the housing industry has lagged or that he can't find decent craftsmen?

Joe needs to take a serious look at his operation and decide what he has under his control that he can change to improve it and make it worth his while or he needs to get out before his meager profits turn into major losses.

Up to this point Joe's strategy has been to spend more to advertise more to bring in more customers. It seems like a hopeless task at times because Joe feels that to turn his current $10,500 profit into his goal of $50,000 per year he would have to turn his 1,000 customer base into almost 5,000 customers.

That means that he would have to work that much harder – but there are only so many hours in the week and so much money in the bank so how can he do that?

What if Joe could not just double or triple but even quadruple his profits or more without having to triple his number of customers, without having to work 100 hours a week?

What if Joe could turn his business into a <u>Profit Machine</u>?

Bibliography

AMEX. (2012). Global Customer Experience Barometer.

Bhasin, K. (2011, 11 22). Retrieved from Business Insider: http://www.businessinsider.com/london-baker-makes-102000-cupcakes-groupon-deal-2011-11

Brown, C. M. (2011, 04 25). www.inc.com. Retrieved from Inc.com: http://www.inc.com/guides/201104/10-pros-cons-for-using-groupon.html

Carnegie, D. (1936). How to Win Friends and Influence People.

Duhigg, C. (2012). The Power of Habit: Why We Do What We Do in Life and Business. Random House.

Gerrard, N. (2012, 02 17). TheCaterer.com/articles/342491. Retrieved from The Caterer.com: https://www.thecaterer.com/articles/342491/research-shows-upselling-is-vital-for-many-businesses

Grethel, P. (2011, 10 17). The Seven Steps of a Sale. Retrieved from Slideshare.Net: http://www.slideshare.net/pjgrethel/seven-steps-of-a-sale

Hill, N. (1937). Think and Grow Rich.

Investopedia. (n.d.). Pareto Principle. Retrieved from Investopedia.com: http://www.investopedia.com/terms/p/paretoprinciple.asp

Katie Smith Milway, C. V. (2005). Bain & Co. Editorial Team

Ken Blanchard, S. J. (1982). The One Minute Manager. HarperCollins.

Macdonald, M. (2012). Shopify.com. Retrieved from Shopify.com: http://www.shopify.ca/blog/8484093-why-online-retailers-are-losing-67-45-of-sales-and-what-to-do-about-it

Mamet, D. (1992). Glengarry Glen Ross.

Natural Marketing Institute (NMI). (2008, March). Understanding the LOHAS Market Report. Retrieved from andeeknutson.com/: http://andeeknutson.com/studies/ LOHAS/General%20Health%20and%20Wellness/11_LOH AS_Whole_Foods_Version.pdf

Ottawa Insight. (2014). Hot Competition. Retrieved from Carlton University Journalism: http://www.cusjc.ca/ ottawainsight/?p=2519

Pink, D. (2012). To Sell Is Human: The Surprising Truth About Motivating Others. London: Penguin Books.

Rackham, N. (1988). Spin Selling. McGraw Hill.

Securities Industry Association. (n.d.).

Statista. (2012). Statista/Statistics. Retrieved from Statista.com: http://www.statista.com/statistics/232285/reasons-for-online-shopping-cart-abandonment/

WorldPay.com. (2012). WorldPay.com/global/forms. Retrieved from WorldPay.com: https://www.worldpay.com/ global/forms/global-online-shopper-report

You Are Not So Smart. (2011, 10 05). The Benjamin Franklin Effect. Retrieved from youarenotsosmart.com: http://youarenotsosmart.com/2011/10/05/the-benjamin-franklin-effect/

Ziglar, Z. (1984). Secrets of Closing the Sale. New York: Berkley.

Index

Recommended Books

Books on Sales and Persuasion

Dale Carnegie, How to Win Friends and Influence People

Robert Cialdini, Influence: The Psychology of Persuasion, 2007

Stephen Covey, The 7 Habits of Highly Effective People: Powerful Lessons in Personal Change, 2004

Matthew Dixon & Brent Adamson, The Challenger Sale: Taking Control of the Customer Conversation, 2011

Thomas Freese, Secrets of Question Based Selling: How the Most Powerful Tool in Business Can Double Your Sales Results, 2000

Joe Girard, Robert L. Shook, Robert Casemore, How to Close Every Sale, 1989

Jeffrey Gitomer, Little Red Book of Selling: 12.5 Principles of Sales Greatness, 2004

Napoleon Hill & Arthur Pell, Think And Grow Rich

Tom Hopkins, How to Master the Art of Selling, 2005

Og Mandino, The Greatest Salesman in the World, 1983

Daniel H. Pink, To Sell Is Human: The Surprising Truth About Moving Others, 2012

Sun Tzu, The Art Of War, originally pub. Around 500 BCE

Brian Tracy, The Psychology of Selling: Increase Your Sales Faster and Easier Than You Ever Thought Possible 2006

Zig Ziglar, Secrets of Closing the Sale, 1984

About the Author

Larry's motto is "Take the road less travelled." After earning his Ph.D. in Chemistry from Georgia Tech he built a lab for a flavor and fragrance company (where he also became responsible for manufacturing the flavoring for Fresca) earning two patents for a process used to manufacture additives to be used at Savannah River Nuclear Plant to remove radionuclides from the waste stored in the leaking underground storage tanks there.

He moved on to running chemical plants, learning Chemical Engineering on-the-job, as Operations Manager as well as Project Manager, Lab Manager, Quality, Safety & Environmental Manager, ran the Tank Farm, Packaging & Shipping and was Emergency Response Team Leader. He was responsible for implementation of an SAP Enterprise Resource Planning system and led a successful ISO 9002 Quality Management System reregistration for his plant site. During that time he earned an MBA from Pepperdine University.

When the Montreal Protocol environmental regulations caused his plant to be shut down he moved from Los Angeles to Victoria, BC in Canada where he bought a restaurant & sold it, bought a franchise business & sold it and was a financial advisor. He is currently a business coach and consultant and an adjunct professor teaching online business courses. He lives in Victoria with his teenage son where he hikes, reads and writes & blogs about business.